Management–
How To Do It

Management– How To Do It

John and Shirley Payne

Gower

Published by
Gower Publishing Limited
Gower House
Croft Road
Aldershot
Hampshire GU11 3HR
England

Gower
Old Post Road
Brookfield
Vermont 05036
USA

John Payne and Shirley Payne have asserted their right under the Copyright, Designs and Patents Act 1988 to be identified as the authors of this work.

British Library Cataloguing in Publication Data

Payne, John
    Management – how to do it
    I. Title II. Payne, Shirley
    658

ISBN 0 566 08094 X

Typeset in 9.5 point Century Old Style by Cappella, Stowmarket and printed in Great Britain by Biddles Ltd, Guildford.

Contents

A note of thanks

We would like to thank all of those people – too numerous to mention individually – who, over many years, have discussed their own management philosophies with us and given us ideas to supplement our own.

Thanks also to Malcolm Stern of Gower who has once again provided useful ideas and advice from the original idea for the book through to its completion.

Finally, our thanks to you for buying the book. We hope that you will enjoy reading it and that the ideas it contains will help you to become an even better manager.

Introduction

Bob: 'Morning, Karen; have a chair. A bit of good news for you. As you know from the Annual Review discussion we had last week, our director Jane and I have been extremely pleased with your performance over the last couple of years. We have decided to set up a new department to handle major accounts and feel that you are the person to run it. So, as of next Monday, I am delighted to say you are the Major Accounts Manager. We are going to transfer Mary, Shavindra, and Karl into the department initially, and you can then add further people as needs dictate. You deserve this: order your new car straight away.'

Karen: 'Bob, I'm not sure what to say . . . thanks! I knew the new department was on the cards but I wasn't sure who might get the job. I'm thrilled that you've picked me, but I have spent the last six years learning to be a good salesperson. However, I'm not being negative when I say I know nothing really about managing other people . . .'

Bob: 'Don't worry! You're good with people. Like me, you'll pick it up as you go along. You can handle it!'

Karen: 'I expect I will cope, but it would be useful to have some sort of straightforward 'How to' guide, you know, so that I can perform well as a manager quickly and avoid the pitfalls that I don't even know about yet.'

*That is precisely what this book is
intended to be!*

However, the book is *not* written just for new or aspiring managers: it should prove useful for experienced managers as well. 'But I am an experienced manager, you reply. Why do I need to read a book like this when I have been doing the job for five years?' Fair question, but think for a minute about driving. Over time we learn, certainly, but we also tend to pick up bad driving habits, don't we? Learning to manage can be like that. This book should help you to check on your current management practices and could perhaps help you to remember some points you had perhaps forgotten, or suggest some ideas that you had not previously considered.

We don't pretend that all of the ideas in this book are new. However, what we have tried to do is to emphasize those ideas, both old and new, **which really do make a difference**. You are almost certain to find that you have met at least a few of our proposals before. Even then, you might not have seen them in quite the way we have described them.

You might also think that some suggestions are simply 'common sense', or 'obvious'. Why, then, doesn't every manager carry them out? Common sense develops in part from encountering a situation, dealing with it, and therefore knowing what to do in a similar situation in the future. 'Common sense' in a managerial context comes primarily from experience – artificial or real. To know that something 'makes common sense', it helps to have been there!

The 80:20 rule

If you don't already know this rule, it states that you will often find an (approximately) 80:20 ratio between related factors. For example:

- 80 per cent of the sales revenue derives from 20 per cent of the customers.

- 80 per cent of the problems are caused by 20 per cent of the people.

- 80 per cent of the results come from 20 per cent of the activities.

Vast amounts of information exist outlining what a manager should and should not do. In fact, there is so much information it is very difficult for someone who wants to learn to know where to start. And even when you know where to look, no one can learn everything. The principal objective must therefore be to identify those ideas that will produce the bulk of the results – and that is an application of the 80:20 rule.

From our twenty-odd years' experience in providing training and development in various management skills, we believe that the ideas contained in this book represent the crucial 20 per cent of ideas that will produce 80 per cent of the results expected from a manager. These ideas alone will not guarantee success, but using them should significantly increase your chances of achieving it!

The objectives of this book

After reading this book, you should know and understand:

- Your strengths and areas for improvement in the various management skills covered by this book.

- The key 20 per cent of ideas that will produce 80 per cent of the results expected of a manager.

How you might use this book

You could just read through the whole book from start to finish, or simply dip into it at random. Either method is fine, but you might prefer a little more direction than that. To help you decide which chapters will give you the best personal reward, and to save you wasting time on what is not essential for you own purposes, we have devised a brief questionnaire. The questionnaire follows this section and should enable you to estimate both your present **level of ability** in the management skills covered by the book and the **importance** of each skill in your job.

New managers (or those developing towards this role)

We suggest that you complete the questionnaire, and then read the whole book starting with the skills that you consider are important to you.

Experienced managers

Complete the questionnaire in order to determine the important areas for you then read only the relevant chapters.

Management skills evaluation questionnaire

This questionnaire should help you, first, to define the management skills that are important in the job you are doing, and secondly, to indicate your existing level of skill in the various areas. Once you have completed the questionnaire, we recommend that you review your answers with your own boss, who should be able to provide useful feedback.

The rating scales

The importance of the skill in the job

Skill	Commentary
H = high	This skill is vital for success
M = medium	Aspects of this skill are necessary, but not vital
L = low	Aspects of this skill are merely helpful
NR = not required	This skill is not needed

Try to avoid the natural tendency to rate every skill as 'high'. At first sight, people tend to think that all skills are important. Indeed they are, but not in *every* job situation. For example, decision making would be a vital skill for a director, but it might be of relatively low importance to, say, a computer operator.

Your existing level of skill

Rating	Commentary
1	Proficient in all aspects of this skill
2	Proficient in some aspects of this skill, but development is required
3	Need to acquire this skill
NR = no requirement	No need at this point to acquire this skill

Do be honest with yourself! We each have our strengths and weaknesses – no one is all 'good' or all 'bad'. Try to be objective and look at yourself, as it were, from outside.

Skills and their definitions

	Importance in the job	Your level of skill
How to determine the results you need (Chapter 1) The ability to define clear, measurable, challenging but realistic results with deadlines for achievement.		
How to plan in order to achieve those results (Chapter 1) The ability to specify how an objective will be achieved, stating or agreeing who will do what by when, and effectively anticipating potential difficulties, but being able to change or adapt plans when required.		
How to make your day more productive (Chapter 2) The ability to analyse information in order to recognize key issues, set and review priorities, and make effective use of available time.		
How to identify why something is happening (Chapter 3) The ability to discover the root cause(s) of why something is 'off-track', so as to permit effective remedial action.		
How to make 'logical' decisions (Chapter 4) The ability to choose between various options, using sound judgement rather than bias.		

	Importance in the job	Your level of skill
How to make 'creative' decisions (Chapter 4) The ability to generate a wide range of creative (novel) solutions and then evaluate their suitability.		
How to communicate orally (Chapter 5) The ability to communicate orally, listen effectively, and handle conflict.		
How to persuade (Chapter 5) The ability to influence/ persuade others (and gain commitment).		
How to lead your team to achieve the results you need (Chapter 6) The ability to achieve results through others, selecting the appropriate style for the situation.		
How to motivate your team (Chapter 6) The ability to create in others a willingness and commitment to achieve the best performance of which they are capable.		

	Importance in the job	Your level of skill

How to delegate (Chapter 7)
The ability to trust a part of the manager's job to someone else, together with the responsibility for its achievement, and the necessary authority to carry it out.

How to present ideas and proposals (Chapter 8)
The ability to present facts/opinions/proposals in a logical and clear way that creates and maintains interest, to achieve the level of understanding required, to handle questions effectively, and, if it is a proposal, to prove the case and secure approval.

How to run an effective meeting (Chapter 9)
The ability to establish the specific results to be achieved, set a suitable structure, effectively involve the participants, and ensure that the outcomes are clear and acceptable.

	Importance in the job	Your level of skill
How to help your people improve their performance (Chapter 10) The ability to help a subordinate identify, explore and 'own' his or her performance strengths and weaknesses, reinforcing strengths and correcting weaknesses, in order to achieve or maintain a higher level of performance.		
How to run an effective appraisal (Chapter 11) The ability objectively to review past performance, and to discuss/agree objectives for the coming period. (Some organizations also include career development in this discussion.)		

Conclusions

From your ratings above:

- What are your key strengths?

- What are your key areas for improvement?

- Which chapters do you need to read?

Chapter summaries

At the end of each chapter, you will find a summary of the ideas contained in that chapter. You may find this summary helpful if you are faced by a situation in which you will need to use the particular skill covered in that chapter and would like a quick reminder. You might even find it helpful to refer to the summary during proceedings, if appropriate.

There is also space after each summary for you to make brief notes of the points you wish to remember after reading the chapter.

1 How to determine what results you need — and achieve them

To be an effective manager, we have to achieve results! In order to do that, we must first clearly define those results and then decide how we are going to accomplish them, and that means setting objectives and planning.

The objectives for this chapter

After reading this chapter, you should know and understand:

- What 'objective setting' and 'planning' are.
- Why objective setting and planning are important and interlinked.
- Some principles that will help you to set objectives for yourself and others, and to plan.

Objective setting, and why it is important

Objective setting can be defined as: 'Identifying and defining the specific results required'. Objectives are important because unless you know where you are going, the likelihood is that you will end up somewhere else. Have you ever been given a vague 'objective' and been told later that you had not done what was required? Whose fault was that?

In our view, the ability to establish and define effective result-oriented objectives is central to good management. It should underlie everything a manager does. All the effective managers we have met know clearly where they are going, even though they may at times be unsure as to the best way to get there. They decide what the future should look like and work with their team to make that vision a reality.

It is also important to separate objectives from aims. An aim is 'a general intention' and is not as specific as an objective. For example, a production manager might have the *aim* of 'improving the quality of widgets produced as the reject rate is too high'. That is an intention. An *objective*, however, might be, say, 'to reduce the reject rate on widgets from 6 per cent to 3 per cent within six months without recruiting additional inspection staff'. The aim has now been turned into a specific result, to be achieved.

Planning, and why it is important

The objective sets out where we are going, while the plan defines *how we are going to get there*.

One approach is to say, 'We have our objective, so let's just get on with it'. But that can easily result in duplication of effort, or in an important task being missed because everybody thought someone else was doing it. Planning is therefore required. An old saying goes, 'If you want to eat an elephant, cut it up'. Thus a plan subdivides the work and ensures that resources are used effectively.

Decide the key results areas initially

IDEA 1

The Problem

'They call me a manager now and I know that I must get results, but *where do I start?*'

An office manager knows that he or she must send invoices out on time; a production manager knows that he or she must move finished products out of the door – but is that all there is to it? Of course not! To avoid a blinkered approach to the situation, in addition to the primary purpose of the department a few indicators are needed to help decide *where* results are required.

The Solution

Start by asking yourself 'What am I here for?' and jot down your thoughts on paper. At this stage just your initial thoughts will be sufficient. Then look at the following list of 'key results areas' and decide in which of these areas you have to achieve results. We have given examples for each area. You may not have entries under each one, however, and in fact after looking at the list you might well pick out other areas that are important to you in your role.

Key results area	Examples
● Primary role	● Meet/exceed sales revenue targets
● Productivity	● Delivery times could be reduced

Key results area	*Examples*
● Quality	● Fewer errors on invoices
● People	● Reduce lateness
● Finance	● Travel costs are high
● Administration	● Some reports are not needed
● Training and development	● Develop Ken into 'deputy' role
● New ideas	● Scrap useless procedures
● Customers	● Find out how they see us
● Special projects (one-offs)	● Set up information database

Focus on results rather than on activities

The Problem

Most managers set objectives (or have them set by their manager). However, if you look at a 'typical' list of objectives, a basic flaw appears with monotonous regularity. They are focused on a series of activities, rather than on the results to be achieved. Some examples include: 'Investigate the production shortfall'; 'Ensure that staff are adequately trained and developed'; 'Prepare a recommendation on departmental staffing' – these are all activities!

There is also a related problem – gobbledegook verbs! 'Optimize productivity ratios for the benefit of the organization' or 'Maximize staff morale'. Looks good (maybe) but means nothing. What do 'optimize' or 'maximize' really mean? People often use these words in this context because they have no idea what can realistically be achieved, or can't be bothered to decide.

The Solution

Setting results-oriented objectives
Objectives are much more positively stated as results, and are clearer as well.

The first question should be: '*Why* am I saying we need to investigate productivity (or whatever)?' This question usually indicates that you must change the focus from an activity into a result. For example, 'We need to investigate productivity to find out why there is a 10 per cent shortfall on product X and then correct that shortfall within a week.'

The second question is: 'Have I now clearly identified the actual result I need?'

Avoiding gobbledegook verbs

Simple – neither use such verbs yourself nor accept them from others! (Blame us if you like for preaching anarchy.) If someone tries to use 'optimize' or 'maximize', ask them what they would regard as a realistic target, or propose the target yourself. Demonstrate the benefit of doing it your way.

Objectives should make their MARC

IDEA 3

The Problem

Too many so-called 'objectives' are too generalized to be of real use. For example, 'Improve the sales of Product X'. The team members responsible for selling 'Product X' then work hard and effect a 10 per cent improvement in sales. Very pleased with themselves, they troop into the boss's office expecting praise, but they could be greeted with: 'Only 10 per cent? I expected at least 15 per cent, and that should have been achieved two months ago!' So what goes wrong?

The person – usually the manager – who is setting the objective probably knows very clearly what he or she means, but the question is whether the people who have actually to achieve the objective understand what is required.

The Solution

A small mnemonic – MARC – might help you remember the essential factors in a well-stated objective:

1 **Measurable** An objective should be measurable to ensure that the person knows when he or she has achieved it. Some things are easy to measure, others are less easy. The 'measurement' you agree might therefore have to be fairly subjective: for example, 'Provide an adequate personnel service to internal customers', which could be measured by asking those customers periodically about the service.

7

2 Achievable It should be seen as achievable by the person who is going to carry it out. One person's 'challenge' might be another's 'impossibility' if their respective levels of skill or knowledge are markedly different.

3 Result-orientated Try to ensure that objectives are stated as results, not activities (see Idea 1.2). Part of the 'result' relates to the deadline by which the objective is to be achieved.

4 Clear The objective must be understood (and agreed) by the person who will have responsibility for achieving it.

So an objective should be *Measurable, Achievable, Result-oriented*, and *Clear* and should include the deadline by which the result has to be achieved.

Prioritize to ensure that effort goes into the important matters

IDEA 4

The Problem

Have you ever found yourself in a situation where you have several things to do, but you know that in the time available you cannot attend to all of them satisfactorily?

We call that 'a clash of priorities', and often the problem is that all the matters to be attended to are so-called priorities. 'Look, boss', you say, 'I'm not going to complete all of these tasks today. Which is the most important?' – to which the boss's reply of 'They *all* are!' is not too helpful. Have you come across the song title 'I want it all and I want it now' by Queen? We know some managers who should have it framed on the wall behind their desks!

When such a clash occurs, therefore, the person either has to make a 'best guess' or check again with their manager (or whoever). But this problem can be eliminated, or at least reduced.

The Solution

Very few lists of objectives show their relative priorities. Yet when discussing a list of objectives it is a simple addition to include a column headed 'Priority' and to rate each objective as 'high', 'medium', or 'low' in that column. Bear in mind that 'low' does not mean 'unimportant'; it just means less important than the 'mediums' or 'highs'.

In the event of a clash of priorities, the 'highs' automatically take precedence and, most of the time, there should be no need for the matter to be referred back to you, as manager.

One final point to note is that priorities of ongoing objectives can alter over time, so it is a good idea to review priority ratings regularly.

Encourage your team to suggest their own objectives

The Problem

Some managers believe that the only person who should set objectives for the team is the manager. These objectives are handed down – rather like the two tablets of stone given to Moses on Mount Sinai – with little opportunity for discussion. There are two reasons behind this thinking:

1 'It's my responsibility as the manager.'

2 'If I ask them to do it, they will set themselves "easy" objectives that won't achieve what I need.'

Examining the first reason, you are certainly responsible for ensuring that the objective is set, but that doesn't necessarily mean that *you* have to set it. The second reason is a natural fear, but is usually unfounded! Most people like a challenge and, if asked, will usually suggest challenging but realistic objectives for themselves.

The Solution

Generally speaking, you need commitment to the objectives (rather than simple acceptance). The best way of ensuring this commitment is to involve the team members in setting their objectives.

Prior to any discussion of objectives, ask them to think first about the key results areas in their job and then to suggest objectives for the coming period for discussion with you. It will also help if you explain MARC (see Idea 1.3) to them if necessary.

The discussion then becomes an exchange of views – yours and theirs. Wherever possible, agree to their proposed objective if it meets the needs that you have and is realistic for them. If their objective does not meet requirements, you need to explain (and prove) why, so that they learn for next time.

Don't try to plan everything – only the key 20 per cent

IDEA 6

The Problem

Have you ever worked with someone who appears to spend most of their time planning what to do, rather than actually doing it? They seem to have plans for absolutely everything, even replacement dates for the pencils in the stationery cupboard! Interestingly, far more detail seems to go into the little plans than into the big ones.

We all accept that planning is important, but if you try to plan everything you would probably end up with mountains of paper that are of little real use in management terms, while having little time to do anything else.

The Solution

Plan the important 20 per cent – that 20 per cent which matters most.

Comprehensive plans should exist for all objectives that relate to key result areas. The plan should clearly show the main tasks necessary for achievement of the objective – tasks that will cause the plan to fail unless they are successfully completed. Taking the example of moving house, 'arranging a removal firm' would be a primary task, while 'arranging for the electricity meter to be read' would not. More planning effort would therefore go into booking the removal firm because if they fail to turn up, you can't move. Failure to have the electricity meter read does not stop you moving.

Make someone responsible for each task, and set a deadline

The Problem

Have a look at a couple of the plans you have. In addition to essential tasks showing *what* should be done:

- Do they also show *who* is responsible for the various tasks?

- Do they show the *deadline* for each task?

If so, you don't need this idea.

However, many plans do not show these important elements. In fact, sometimes the people who have to carry out the plan aren't even given a copy! (Another idea?)

Without specific responsibilities, confusion can easily arise . . . 'I thought you were doing that part!'

Without specific deadlines for each main task, the whole plan can easily slip behind and then fail to achieve the original objective.

The Solution

For each specific task:

- Decide and agree a single person who will be responsible for ensuring that that particular task is successfully achieved. Joint responsibilities are risky, for they can lead to confusion.

- Decide and agree the deadline by which that task must be successfully completed.

As the individual selected will have responsibility for ensuring that the task is both completed and completed on time, their commitment is usually vital. So agree the objectives with them at the planning stage.

Spot the time bombs

The Problem

Most people don't have a problem planning how to do something. The difficulty centres around making the plan *work,* that is, successfully completing all of the plan's component parts so that the overall objective is achieved.

The plan says what should happen, but ask yourself how many of your plans go right from start to finish?

We are convinced there is a band of 'planning gremlins' whose sole aim in life is to wreck even the most brilliant plans. They have the ability to place time bombs just where they will do most damage, and they do!

'But hang on', you say, 'I agree, but I can't anticipate everything, can I?' No, but some people don't seem to anticipate *anything,* even obvious time bombs (for example, where they have been caught out before). They have this blind faith in their ability to handle anything as and when it arises. So why, then, do some of their plans still not work?

The Solution

Accept reality (or the existence of 'planning gremlins') and accept that it is better to anticipate and deal with the most serious time bombs, rather than simply to wait for them to explode. By recognizing them at the planning stage you may be able to decide what can be done to pre-handle them. The minor potential time bombs probably don't cause you too much lost sleep. Even if they go off, the damage would be minimal and easily handled.

There are those, of course, who see this search for potential time bombs as somehow negative, and no one likes to be called negative. Locating these timebombs, however, is the first step towards defusing them! Thus it is, in fact, a very positive approach, aimed at removing the problems that can potentially ruin the plan.

Prevent fires, rather than fight them

IDEA 9

The Problem

In Idea 1.8, we referred to the need to search for the potential time bombs that can (and do) ruin even the best plans. This idea concerns what we should do about these time bombs when we find them.

Some people seem to be terrific fire-fighters. They come into their own when there is a crisis, and are seen by some as Mr (or Ms) Fixit. Now there is a lot of good publicity in fire-fighting if it is done successfully. Fixit rushes in with the fire extinguisher and the building is saved with minimum damage. Hooray for Fixit!

So the Fixits of the world thrive, and, OK, the fire is out. But the question still remains, should that fire have been allowed to start in the first place? Frequently the answer is that it should not! All that was needed was some initial thought about potential causes.

As it is impossible, though, to anticipate everything, so it is equally impossible to prevent everything. How do you stop a key member of the team going sick at a critical stage of the project? You probably can't! So what should you do?

The Solution

Having defined the chief sources of potential problems:

● Decide on actions to prevent those which are realistically preventable. For example, possible board rejection of a proposal might be prevented by finding out beforehand what the directors' criteria are.

● Decide what fire-fighting actions should be taken for those problems that you cannot prevent. For example, to lessen the impact of a project leader going absent (for whatever reason) at a critical stage, ensure that he or she nominates a deputy at the start, who will take over in the leader's absence.

Control the key 20 per cent of tasks in a plan

The Problem

As we mentioned in Idea 1.6, the planning of the key 20 per cent is most important. It is equally important to *control* that 20 per cent.

Trying to control everything is an impossible task, yet some people try! There are also managers who are continually checking – on everything. Interestingly, they seem to concentrate more on the really minor issues – changing one totally unimportant word in a report, for example – rather than on the important things! Maybe it looks good (and is easier). Have you noticed this type of behaviour?

The Solution

You can't control everything, so make sure you do control the key 20 per cent that will produce 80 per cent of the results you need. To aid control, ensure that, if possible, the information is permanently visible, rather than buried in some dusty old filing cabinet (or even in the depths of some dusty high-tech. computer).

A sales director we knew had a very simple graph on his office wall. One line showed 'Sales revenue', the other line, 'Cost of sales'. Next to the graph he placed the most recent letter from a customer – complimentary or otherwise. In his view, these factors represented the key 20 per cent.

And the first item on the agenda of his regular sales management meetings was always to review these factors and decide appropriate actions.

Summary

How to determine what results you need

- Decide the key results areas initially.
- Focus on results rather than on activities.
- Objectives should make their MARC.
- Prioritize to ensure that effort goes into the important matters.
- Encourage your team to suggest their own objectives.

How to achieve those results

- Don't try to plan everything – only the key 20 per cent.
- Make someone responsible for each task, and set a deadline.
- Spot the time bombs.
- Prevent fires, rather than fight them.
- Control the key 20 per cent of tasks in a plan.

Points to remember:

_____

_____

_____

_____

_____

_____

_____

2 How to make your day more productive

Some people rush from one crisis to another: they are late for appointments and meetings, forget to do things, and are never available when you need them. Others seem to have life, both at work and at home, better organized. They accomplish much, yet still seem to be able to find the time to sit and talk! How do they do it? An old adage states: 'If you want something done, give it to the busy person.' We would change 'busy' to 'effective', two terms that do not necessarily mean the same thing.

The ideas in this chapter will not make you the perfect time-manager, but they could help you to organize your time more effectively and still be able to deal with the unexpected.

The objectives for this chapter

After reading this chapter, you should know and understand:

- Why personal time management is so important.
- Some principles that will help you to manage your time effectively.

Time management

In this context we have defined time management as: 'making the most productive use out of the time we spend at work'. Some of the ideas apply equally well, of course, to home life.

Why managing our time is important

Are there ever enough hours in the day to do everything you would like? Well, the 35-hour day has yet to be discovered. Whatever we do, there are only 24 hours in a day, and the challenge is to make the best use of them. We have to ensure that what should be done actually is done, and that, realistically, we are also still able to cope with the (unexpected) extras which come along, and which often seem to be designed specifically to wreck our plans.

Your own attitude is the most important factor

The Problem

Most people have at least some difficulty in managing their time. When difficulties arise, it is the easiest thing in the world to start apportioning blame:

- 'They moved the goal posts on me, again!'

- 'He always wants everything yesterday.'

- 'If only I wasn't interrupted every five minutes, I could actually do some work!'

- 'I've spent the whole day answering the phone.'

We all do it, but have you noticed how easy it is to blame *everyone* or *everything else* for *our* difficulty in handling our *own* time?

'So are you saying that it is all my own fault, then?' No. People we work with and the job we do all make demands on our time, but 'blame' doesn't really solve anything! It might make us feel better, but it doesn't *change* anything, does it?

The Solution

We firmly believe that the solution to effective time management lies in *our own attitude* towards the problems. People who have difficulty with time management will be 90 per cent towards solving their problem when they are prepared to say: 'Much of this is really my fault. I let it happen! The other factors just contribute to it.'

No improvement is likely, however, unless we understand that our time management is our own problem, and that the only person who can positively change anything on this score is ourself.

We may not be able easily to change the habits and practices of others. Ask yourself, however, what *you* do (or don't do) that contributes to the problem? What are *you* prepared to do about it, and *by when* will you do it? Try noting a few ideas down now.

Any system is fine as long as it is yours

IDEA 2

The Problem

There is a train of thought which maintains that by spending upwards of £100 on a sophisticated time management system – leather-bound, or computerized – time management problems can be solved at a stroke. Sadly . . . no!

We are not against systems as such. Indeed we use one system that is effective for us. Nevertheless, any system you employ must suit you and the way you want to work. The problem is that all too often these systems force you into doing things *their* way, which may not achieve what you want, or are so complicated that you seem to spend all day planning what to do that day. Consequently, either only a small part of the system is actually used, or the system is not used at all.

The Solution

Any 'system' is fine as long as it suits you, but it is worth stressing that some sort of system, however simple, is necessary to inject order into our day. If writing a 'To do' list on the back of a cigarette packet works for you, then do that. Likewise, if using a very expensive leather-bound system makes you feel good and spurs you to manage your time more effectively, that's fine too.

But if your present 'system' leaves something to be desired, first, jot down what any new 'system' must do for you. Then, and only then, look at the available options, including that of modifying your existing system.

Finally, it is worth noting that those who use computerized time management systems usually find they have to carry a diary/notebook as well – desktop computers aren't too portable! There is therefore some duplication, with two systems running together.

'Urgent' is not necessarily 'important'

IDEA 3

The Problem

It's amazing how easily we confuse 'urgent' with 'important'.

What happens when the phone rings? Yes, we answer it, sure we do! Telephones seem to have a way of instilling a feeling of urgency . . . the insistent ringing, and so forth. The phone *should* be answered. That isn't the problem. The problem hinges on what follows. For instance, have you ever answered the phone and then spent the next hour trying to deal with some 'urgent' but minor issue – often for someone else?

Simply because something is urgent, it doesn't necessarily follow that it is also important! Yet, urgent items always seem to gain priority, because if we leave them we know that deadlines will be missed and so on.

However, if urgent items constantly stop you dealing with the important matters, ask yourself how you will be viewed by your own boss!

The Solution

First, try not simply to *react* to pressure over an urgent item. Add it to your 'To do' list and prioritize it (high, medium, or low), based on both 'urgency' and 'importance'. Deal with other items in the same way, remembering that:

- High *urgency* is the need for something to be done immediately.

- High *importance* is that which relates to a crucial objective – that is, it has a real impact.

Then look at your 'To do' list and decide in what order the various tasks should be done. How should you be spending your time *now*?

The tasks that are high on both urgency and importance are done immediately and the necessary time is spent on them. Items that are urgent but unimportant should be done quickly, but without the need to spend much time on them. It might help to set a time limit for each item.

Put your 'To Do' list in your diary

IDEA 4

The Problem

'To do' lists would be a wonderful invention, if only they didn't seem to grow faster than we can reduce them. A friend of ours maintains that all 'To do' lists ought to be written on a roll of toilet paper because they just get longer and longer. A frightening thought, but he has a point!

Most people keep some sort of list of things to do – in a book, on sheets of A4, on 'Post-it' notes, and so forth. Not only can these become cumbersome, they can also be lost all too easily. 'I had a little note about that here somewhere.' . . . searching frantically through mounds of paper.

The Solution

Consider putting the things you have to do *straight into your diary*, along with appointments and meetings. This approach has two advantages:

1 The list is less likely to be mislaid – unless you lose your diary!

2 By assigning the tasks to particular days they are more visible (we usually look at a diary at least daily), and they are more likely to be done when they should be done, rather than left to the last minute.

'But what if I don't do, or finish, something?' Write it into the next available day. Duplication irritates so there is a built-in motivation to get it done, rather than keep rewriting some task or other.

As you finish each task, tick it or cross it off. That action alone gives a feeling of accomplishment, and also reminds you what there is left to do that day.

Don't rush around aimlessly – organize a routine day

The Problem

Have you noticed how some people appear to be more organized than others? They react immediately to every call on their time – the latest demand is always the one to tackle right now. However, what we *should* be doing is often different from what we actually *are* doing!

Certainly there are those who enjoy reacting immediately, 'firing from the hip', but while that might give the odd adrenaline 'rush', it is not necessarily effective! Most of us enjoy some 'sensible' pressure and often feel that we perform best under these circumstances. What happens, though, if that pressure becomes permanent? It either becomes normal so it ceases to have the motivational effect, or it puts us into stress 'overload'. Neither is very effective.

There are, in most jobs, a series of routine tasks that must be done regularly: for example, read the mail, check and sign the expenses, prepare the monthly report, and so on. These tasks are sometimes (often?) fairly boring. Some of us look for any excuse to be doing something far more interesting and enjoyable, and reacting to demands can seem a justifiable way of doing so . . . 'Sorry, I didn't finish the report as I spent most of the day helping Jane with that computer problem she has.' The truth is we enjoyed dealing with the problem more than writing the report, so the routine matter suffers.

The Solution

Spend the first ten minutes of your working day deciding which tasks you *must* do in that eight hours and which you would *like* to do, if there is time.

If appropriate, plan to do the routine (boring) items first. Having completed those, then reward yourself with something interesting or enjoyable as the next task.

Don't wait for the unexpected – allow for it!

The Problem

At first sight, this might look similar to the last idea (Idea 2.5). In one sense, it is. Both ideas concern planning your day. In Idea 2.5 we were talking about someone who does very little planning; in this idea we are talking about someone who plans too much!

Assuming that you already try to plan your day in some way, consider one of your recent daily plans and ask yourself whether you completed it. If you only did most of it or some of it, why was that?

The most likely reason we have found for non-completion is that 'unexpected' demands on your time arose and wrecked the original plan. 'Hold on though. With the best will in the world, I can't plan for the unexpected, can I? It wouldn't be unexpected then.' True, but analyse your daily plan. How much work did you actually plan to do in 8 hours? Many daily plans that people produce appear to allocate something close to 8 hours work to be done in an 8-hour day. In other words, no time is left for the unexpected, and therefore when it does arise the plan is disrupted. Planning to do 8 hours work in 8 hours is unrealistic!

The Solution

One or two hours (maybe even more) of your day are likely to be spent handling the unexpected. You can't plan for the actual tasks that arise, but you can *allocate time* for the unexpected! You might find it useful to keep a rough log for a few days to see how much time you actually spend on these unexpected tasks.

Once you know, on average, how much time the unexpected typically takes, allow for it in your daily plans. Suppose that handling the unexpected takes 2 hours on average, then do not plan any more than 6 hours work for each day. This approach is not perfect but you are more likely to complete your plan in this way because that plan is far more realistic.

IDEA 7

Avoid playing 'desk chess'

The Problem

Does this sound at all familiar? You are going through your in-tray and come to a tricky item and think 'Mmmm, not sure what to do with this one.' So you place it top left on your desk.

Later in the day it is still there and you feel rather guilty. You have a look, and are still unsure what to do with it so you move it to the bottom right . . . 'That's better. At least I have done *something*.'

Eventually after several unproductive moves around the desk, you put it into some secret place (bottom drawer?) reserved for such items and hope nobody asks for it. That is playing 'desk chess'.

The Solution

Several ideas might help:

- Pick out the items with which you play 'desk chess'. Every time you move one of these items round the desk, punch a hole in the top corner. This will soon show you which items are the culprits!

- Indecision – Ask yourself what will happen if you *don't* act. Any decision could be better than none.

- More information is needed. Make that phone call to request the information and put the file in your 'Awaiting reply' tray.

- If the task is just difficult or uninteresting, do it, but reward yourself afterwards with a cup of coffee or something that you enjoy doing.

IDEA 8

Learn how to say 'No' constructively

The Problem

There are people around whom we (and everyone else) love. These are the well-meaning folk who *never* say 'No'. They take on too much and easily go into 'overload'. In short, they are often put upon! They try very hard to do everything they take on, but end up spending most of their time doing things for everyone else and little time on their own work. Certainly they are viewed by other people as helpful and are probably also well liked, but just consider how their boss sees it. Is it any real excuse for not doing your own work to say that you were helping everyone else?

Then there are others who *always* say 'No', and are quite ruthless about it. They probably complete their own work, but are seen by others as decidedly unhelpful and generally to be avoided wherever possible.

Reasons differ for these types of behaviour, but both are equally wrong!

Decide whether you commit either of the 'sins'.

The Solution

Everyone recognizes that we all occasionally have to say 'No' if we are to complete our own work satisfactorily and in time. The correct approach is therefore twofold:

1 Don't say 'No' all of the time.

2 When you do have to say 'No', do it constructively.

Moreover, when a colleague does have a serious problem on some very important task, try to reorganize your schedule in order to help. Check, though, that the situation is definitely critical, and not simply panic on your colleague's part.

If you have shown that you are prepared to help when there is a genuine crisis, it is easier to say 'No' when what you are doing takes priority. Always explain the reasons why you cannot respond when asked for help – that is, the importance or urgency of your own immediate task.

Interrupted by a visitor? . . . Stand up!

The Problem

The 80:20 rule yet again . . . 80 per cent of our interruptions are caused by 20 per cent of the people.

Have you ever been sitting at your desk and seen *him* or *her* heading in your direction and thought, 'Oh no. Not them, not today, PLEASE!' They arrive, grab the nearest chair, make themselves comfy, and you know you are in for a long session!

The difficulty is that until they start to talk, you have no idea how important their subject is. If it is urgent or important, there is probably not any issue – the interruption is valid! However what do you do if they want to discuss the holiday they have just had, but you are desperately trying to prepare a presentation for the MD which is needed in ten minutes? Once they are seated and comfortable, they are very hard to get rid of!

The Solution

The answer is not to let them 'get comfy' until you decide whether their visit is justified. Don't dispose of the visitor's chair (you may need it at some future stage!). Try this instead. As they approach your desk, stand up!

People do not seem prepared to sit next to your desk *whilst you are standing*. At most they might perch on the corner of your desk, which is not too comfortable anyway. You can then say something along the lines of 'Morning, David. What can I do for you?' Their reply should tell you what you need to know. You can then sit them down or suggest talking later.

Why read or write reams unnecessarily? . . . Use the 'Churchill Principle'

IDEA 10

The Problem

Do you spend much time reading or writing reams? If so, you might be able to save yourself considerable time by adopting this idea.

Often, we are looking for only one or two key points. The problem is that, in order to find them, we have to read through umpteen pages, or at least scan the whole document.

A similar situation can apply in reverse. When we are writing a report, we often include much detail and/or justification on the grounds that 'they might need this information'.

The Solution

The first question must of course be: 'Do I need to read/write this anyway?' If not, don't! Too much paper goes to people who don't actually need (or want) it anyway.

However, let's assume that you do need to read or write regular reports. In this case, consider applying the 'Churchill

Principle' (slightly modified): 'Tell me, *on one side of one sheet of paper only,* what I need to know.'

If you are the recipient of regular reports, consider whether a one-sheet summary of key points will tell you what you need to know. If so, tell the author. It will save them time in writing as well. Similarly, if you are going to write a regular report, find out whether a one-sheet summary of key points will be sufficient for the receiver. On odd occasions when more detail is needed as back-up, this can often be provided over the phone.

Summary

Making your day more productive

- Your own attitude is the most important factor.
- Any system is fine as long as it is yours.
- 'Urgent' is not necessarily 'important'.
- Put your 'To Do' list in your diary.
- Don't rush around aimlessly – organize a routine day.
- Don't wait for the unexpected – allow for it!
- Avoid playing 'desk chess'.
- Learn how to say 'No' constructively.
- Interrupted by a visitor? . . . Stand up!
- Why read or write reams unnecessarily? . . . Use the 'Churchill Principle'.

Points to remember

_____

_____

_____

_____

_____

_____

_____

3 How to find out why something is happening

The term 'problem solving' can itself cause problems! People use it to combine two distinct things: finding out why a problem exists, then fixing it. We see these two processes as separate: that is, finding out what is the cause (this chapter) is different from deciding what is the best course of action (Chapter 4).

While decision making *might* follow cause analysis, this does not always apply. You might need to make a decision without any problem as such to solve, for example in deciding whom to promote to manage a new section. Alternatively, you may want to find out why something is happening in a situation where someone else will subsequently have to make the decision about what to do – investigating a situation on behalf of another manager because you have the technical expertise is one example.

The objectives for this chapter

After reading this chapter, you should know and understand:

- Why 'problem solving' should be seen as 'cause analysis'.

- Why problem solving is important.

- Some principles that will help you to find the real cause of a 'problem'.

Problem solving, and why it should be called cause analysis

Chuck Kepner and Ben Tregoe in their book *The New Rational Manager* (1981), defined a 'problem' as: 'a deviation from normal, where the cause is unknown, and you need to know the cause'. In their terms, if you *know* the cause, then you do not have a problem to solve. You might, though, have a decision to make.

The difficulty hinges on the word 'problem'. It is usually seen as negative, that is, something is wrong. A deviation from normal can of course be positive or negative. For example, it is probably just as important to find out why a member of the team is performing so well as it is to find out why, say, the reject rate has gone up. For this reason, we feel that the process could more positively be termed 'cause analysis', rather than 'problem solving', as 'cause analysis' does not put a negative slant on the process.

In this chapter, therefore, we will use the term '**cause analysis**'.

Why cause analysis is important

Often we need to know why something is happening in order to reinforce it (if it is positive) or correct it (if it is negative). At some time we have all probably taken action, only to find later that we were attacking the wrong cause. There is the story about the chap whose car coasted to a stop, and, because the ignition light was on, he replaced the battery – only to find out that he had run out of petrol! You would never do that sort of thing, would you?

Thus, if something is 'off–track', we have to find out exactly why this is happening, so that our actions deal with the real cause rather than assumed ones.

Clearly separate 'cause' from 'effect'

IDEA 1

The Problem

Cause analysis has, by definition, to deal with cause and effect. Sometimes people do not separate cause and effect, or become so confused that they attempt to deal with the effect rather than the cause.

The problem is that a cause is itself an effect of an even deeper cause. Where, then, do you stop? An example might help to illustrate the difficulty:

- The central heating system at home breaks down, which was caused by . . .

- The pump seizing up, which was caused by . . .

- Sludge in the water, which was caused by . . .

- Lack of an inhibitor to stop the sludge, which was caused by . . .

- The plumber not putting inhibitor in, which was caused by . . .

- Poor training of the plumber, and so on.

As you can see, replacing the pump is dealing with the effect, and it would solve the problem only temporarily until the sludge built up again. Our action in this case is too superficial. Yet at the other (lower) end of the problem, you probably can't do much about your plumber's training! The most practical solution, therefore, is to ask a plumber to put an inhibitor in the system and then replace the pump.

The Solution

The question we have to ask is: 'How far do I need to go back to solve this problem for all practical purposes?'

Don't try to solve the world's problems! Be clear about where your responsibility ends and others' begins. Identify those causes of problems on which *you* can take, or initiate, some form of action to eliminate them.

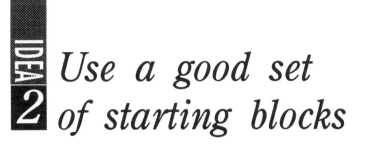

IDEA 2

Use a good set of starting blocks

The Problem

When we are starting to look at a deviation from normal, having a good set of starting blocks – that is, a sound basis to start from – is essential. All too often we generalize far too easily, and even give titles to some of the bigger or longer-term problems: the invoicing problem, the sales problem, the absentee problem, and so on. Everyone believes they know what is meant by each term, but often individuals have very different views that don't always match. Take the 'invoicing problem', for example. The head of administration might see it as a need for more motivated staff to process the invoices quicker; the invoicing manager might see it as a requirement for better computer facilities; the sales manager regards it as the reason why the invoices are often incorrect; while the invoicing clerk looks upon it as management expecting the impossible.

Remember also that a deviation is not merely negative.

The Solution

Setting the starting blocks correctly helps an athlete to avoid false starts or bad starts. The same applies with cause analysis: if the right start is made, the rest becomes easier (you don't have to make up for lost time).

Before trying any detailed analysis, therefore, we have to know exactly what deviation it is we are trying to analyse, and this necessitates asking:

● What or who is involved?

● Exactly what is the deviation from normal?

Thus applying these questions to our 'invoicing problem', we might end up with:

- Invoices under £5,000 are going out fifteen days late.

Define the problem effectively

The Problem

'Effectively' means being systematic about collecting relevant information. Yet often our first step is to note down everything we know about the issue – data about it, possible causes, more data, possible actions, and so forth, all mixed up together.

Cause analysis must be systematic, otherwise there is the danger of going off down blind alleys, only to find – sometimes much later – that we have to return to the main route. Moreover, there is little point in trying to check a possible cause until we have some facts against which to judge whether it is the real cause or not.

The Solution

First, decide if you already know *why* the issue exists. If you are absolutely sure you know the cause, then you don't need cause analysis.

> *I keep six honest serving-men*
> *(They taught me all I knew);*
> *Their names are What and Why and When*
> *And How and Where and Who.*

Rudyard Kipling, *Six Honest Serving-Men*

If you don't know, or are unsure about, the cause, use the remaining five of Kipling's six honest serving-men to guide you in systematically collecting data about the issue.

- What (is happening)?
- When (does it happen)?
- How (does it show up)?
- Where (is it happening)?
- Who (is involved)?

Be specific when defining the problem

The Problem

When collecting data about the deviation (good or bad), people again tend to generalize.

Suppose, for example, there is a problem with invoices going out late. Use of Kipling's six honest serving-men might generate the following answers:

- What? – invoices
- How? – at management meeting
- Why? – not too sure, might be the computer
- Where? – Accounts department
- When? – this quarter
- Who? – Accounts staff

However, this information is far too general to be of much practical use.

The Solution

Be specific when answering the questions yourself! If you are trying to get information from others who are generalizing, try adding the word 'exactly' in front of each question.

- What? – all invoices for furniture over £1,000 going out 10 days late
- How? – reported by invoicing section leader at meeting on 30 March 1997
- Why? – the cause is unknown
- Where? – invoicing section, Accounts department

- When? – since
  1 March this year

- Who? – only those staff in
  the section who deal with
  furniture invoices over
  £1,000.

5 Use charts and diagrams to help

The Problem

When trying to define a 'problem', words alone can be rather restrictive. Sometimes it is far from easy to say what is happening or where it is happening. We have all heard the phrase 'One picture is worth a thousand words'. In the case of cause analysis, a picture or diagram can also *save* a thousand words!

The Solution

Consider whether a chart or diagram will further help to define the problem, by providing additional data.

Occasionally, a chart or diagram can show something that words alone will not describe. For example, in the illustration in this section, the chart shows that the drop in sales was dramatic and instant in June. On the office layout, if the difficulty concerned only the two people at the shaded desks, the diagram might help to generate extra data. Try it!

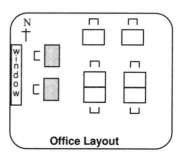

Office Layout

In addition to diagrams, other types of useful charts are:

- Graph (as shown above).

- Bar chart (similar to a graph, but with shaded blocks instead of a plotting line).

- Pie chart (cutting the pie into proportional slices).

- Frequency list (counts the number of times an activity occurs so that the daily/weekly/monthly frequency can be identified).

Don't make unreasonable assumptions, particularly about the cause of 'people' problems

IDEA 6

The Problem

Mark: 'So, some of the team are unhappy about having to work overtime to complete that job, are they? That David has a considerable attitude problem. The guy's motivation is zero and he always manages to wind the team up as well. He can wreck in a day what we have taken a year to build up. He's going to have to go!'

Dawn: 'But, Mark, David is delighted with the prospect of some overtime . . .'

Why do we have this need to find someone to *blame* and, what's more, then to make assumptions to back up our findings? Maybe it's easier than finding out what *really* caused the problem.

You may well have heard the proverb 'Give a dog a bad name and hang him'. We too easily assume that someone with whom we have had difficulties in the past *must* be at the bottom of the problem again this time.

The Solution

We all make assumptions some of the time – you can't check everything. There are *credible* assumptions, and there are *incredible* ones! You have to know whether yours, and others, are credible or incredible.

Cause analysis relies on facts so identify any assumptions in the data and check them to see whether they are correct. On occasions where you cannot check at that point, mark the data in some way to show that it is an assumption rather than fact.

Deviations are caused by changes

The Problem

Having collected the data, we now need to try and identify possible causes of the 'problem'. For any deviation there could be many possibilities.

What typically seems to happen is that people hold a personal or group brainstorming-type session to generate these possibilities, asking: 'What could possibly cause this situation?'

The resulting list can be enormous, and it will take a long time to check each possibility. What is needed is some concept or method that reduces the list of possibilities to those that are likely to have a *direct bearing* on the problem. But how can you generate only those possible causes that might actually have a direct bearing?

The Solution

To ensure that only relevant possible causes are considered, there is a step we must take before trying to generate causes.

This is where Newton's first law of motion comes in, which states 'Every body continues in a state of rest or uniform motion in a straight line unless acted upon by an external impressed force'. In our opinion, this concept is the real key to effective cause analysis. Grasp this concept and you have understood the most significant aspect.

Try to identify what *relevant* changes have occurred at, or around, the time the deviation first arose. It will also help to note when the change occurred. Then you can generate possible causes from these changes. For example, suppose there was a change to a computer system. The possible cause might be: 'the new computer system is faulty, making incorrect calculations'.

Find the real cause

IDEA 8

The Problem

Now you have a list of possible causes. It is fairly unlikely that they all caused the deviation, but how do you decide which causes are at the bottom of the 'problem'?

Occasionally, a problem-solving group will divide into sub-groups and each take a possible cause to check on and report back. Undoubtedly this is a good division of labour, but is it really necessary to spend so much time modifying everything to see the effect?

Alternatively, some groups pick the particular cause that they 'like the look of', and go off to remedy that and see what happens. Fine if they have chosen the right cause, but how much time and money is wasted if they have not found the right one?

What is needed is some method of 'eliminating the impossible', as Sherlock Holmes would say.

> How often have I said to you that when you have eliminated the impossible, whatever remains, however improbable, must be the truth?
>
> Sir Arthur Conan Doyle, *The Sign of Four*

The Solution

If you have used the earlier ideas in this chapter, the solution already exists. All you need to do is use it!

Take each of the possible causes and compare each one with the 'what, why, when, how, where and who' data you collected. Ask whether that cause would explain *all* of the facts you have. For example, say one possible cause is 'new computer system faulty', you might find that the system was changed *after* the problem first arose. That eliminates that cause!

When you have eliminated the impossible via this approach, whatever is left must be the truth!

What if you eliminate *everything*? Either one or more of your facts are wrong, or there has been a change somewhere that you have missed.

Careful – there may be more than one cause!

The Problem

Consider the following problem. Production (of car components) has fallen by 20 per cent. After cause analysis, the production manager was left with several possible causes that could not be entirely eliminated:

● Faulty batch of raw material (metal rods) delivered.

● Quality standards (tolerances on dimensions) now more stringent, causing more scrap.

● Demotivation due to rumours (unfounded) of redundancies in the factory.

● Increased checking by Quality Control increasing reject rate.

All of these causes are relevant but, if they were all under your control, which would you tackle first?

The Solution

Occasionally, you may find that you are left with several causes, as in the example above. It might help to prioritize action by asking the following questions:

● Which is the *root* cause – the one that *directly* produces the problem?

● Which are *contributory* causes – those that contribute to the problem but do not directly cause it?

In the example above, the root cause was more stringent quality standards and they were found to be unrealistic for the relatively old machines in the factory. Consequently, production of 'good' components fell by 20 per cent. The other factors contributed to the problem but did not actually cause it. The rumours and demotivation resulted from the reduced production output, the faulty material only applied to one day's production, and the higher reject rates meant more frequent checking by the inspectors.

Summary

Finding out why something is happening

- Clearly separate 'cause' from 'effect'.
- Use a good set of starting blocks.
- Define the problem effectively.
- Be specific when defining the problem.
- Use charts and diagrams to help.
- Don't make unreasonable assumptions, particularly about the cause of 'people' problems.
- *Deviations are caused by changes* (this is the key concept!).
- Find the real cause.
- Careful – there may be more than one cause!

Points to remember

_____

_____

_____

_____

_____

_____

_____

4 How to make decisions

Decision making is an interesting management skill. Many people seem to think that they don't make many decisions, appearing to associate decision making with *important* decisions only. Certainly we usually give important decisions considerable thought, but probably less than 20 per cent of the decisions we make fall into this catergory. We all make many other decisions – the remaining 80 per cent – in the course of an average day. We just don't perhaps realize it! Often we make these decisions quickly, but that doesn't mean there is *no* thought put into them. It is merely that we use a simpler process (and it should be!).

The ideas in this chapter should help you when making decisions. You will have to decide which ideas apply to the various decisions that you are called upon to make.

The objectives for this chapter

After reading this chapter, you should know and understand:

- The difference between 'logical' and 'creative' decision making.

- Why they are both important.

- Some principles that will help you with both types of decision making.

'Logical' decision making and why it is important

Decisions that we call 'logical' are those where you have a finite number of options from which to choose, and your objective is to select the options that best meet the requirement. For example, choosing a new computer system would fall into this category as would deciding whom to promote or recruit.

The wrong choice would cause problems and the more important the decision, the greater would be the problems. Imagine the costs (direct and indirect) of recruiting the wrong person.

'Creative' decision making and why it is important

We use the term 'creative' to cover those decisions where there are, as yet, no options and the objective is first to *create* them. Having generated possible options, we can then evaluate them in much the same way as for 'logical' decisions. Decisions that fall into this category might include how could we market our services more widely or how could we increase revenue.

'Creative' decisions encourage the generation of *novel* approaches and ideas and are vital where we need to find new, innovative ways to move forward.

Set criteria before *thinking* about the options

IDEA 1

The Problem

Focus on a recent decision you made, and how you made it. Usually you will have started by weighing up the various options available, and then comparing them in order to decide which best suited your purposes.

Is there anything wrong with that? No, nothing . . . that is, unless a serious risk rears its head . . . *bias!*

Have you ever convinced yourself that such and such is the best option solely because you *liked* that particular choice? In fact, you may well have made up your mind unconsciously after seeing the one you like. The rest were effectively a lost cause. In cases like this, we can easily 'bend' the requirements to suit our bias – without even realizing it sometimes. A friend went out to buy a sporty family saloon and came back with a two-seater sports car! His partner 'suggested' he might perhaps need to buy a roof rack for the three kids! After a couple of weeks he changed the car, but it cost him (in more ways than one)!

The Solution

We can't help having biases – we're human! We can, however, avoid bias encouraging us to make the wrong choice. The answer is to set some criteria before even considering any options.

Criteria describe the ideal you are trying to achieve, and it usually helps to categorize these criteria as either 'essential' or 'desirable'. For instance, if you are buying a house, some of the criteria might be: 'I can't afford more than £100,000 so that's essential, and we must have three bedrooms. I would like a place within 15 minutes of the railway station and primary school, and, ideally, it would have character, for example exposed beams.'

Incidentally, there is nothing wrong with including likes and dislikes in your criteria, provided they are appropriate (and legal).

Consider a range of options, including 'stay as we are'

IDEA 2

The Problem

As we mentioned in Idea 4.1, bias can cause us problems. Another aspect of potential bias is unreasonably to limit the options we are able to consider to the one or two that we like, or have worked before. Except for 'yes/no' decisions, there are rarely only a couple of options.

A manifestation of this problem is when you hear yourself (or someone else) saying 'But we have always done it this way'. Fear of the unknown can easily generate *unreasonable* bias against new or different approaches to doing things.

At the other end of the scale, some decision-making discussions never consider the option of 'stay as we are'. However, the way forward should represent an improvement on the current position, but if the current position is *not* considered, how can improvement be measured?

The Solution

Look at the options being generated and ask yourself whether they represent a reasonable *range*, including the option of 'stay as we are'.

IDEA 3

Always consider the risks as well as the benefits

The Problem

Most people look at the benefits of each of the available options when trying to make a decision. Some, however, seem to feel that considering the risks introduces a negative note to the proceedings. Consequently, the risks receive scanty attention – if any! People learn quickly that suggesting possible risks is 'not OK', so it is not too surprising that they keep quiet about them.

Some go the other way. All they appear to do is to make decisions based on the option with the minimum risk, that is, the safe option. While it might be safe, the question is: 'Will that option actually produce the best result?' If there is another option that has higher (though manageable) risks, but far more benefits, then probably not.

The Solution

Good decision making should be objective and that, to us, means considering both the benefits *and the risks* of each option. The perfect option has yet to be invented. Try to consider the severity and likelihood of the risk to indicate its significance.

Decision making is a balancing act – balancing the benefits of each option against the risks. If there is an option with the highest benefits and least snags, the decision is easy. If, on the other hand, there is a high-benefit/high-risk option, ask whether it is possible to reduce or manage those risks in order to achieve the benefits.

Group decisions – use a flipchart to reduce potential conflict

The Problem

Group decision making can easily become highly emotional! One person wants option 1; someone else is strongly in favour of option 2. Not too surprising, then, that the emotional temperature rises when personal judgement is apparently being called into question.

'You always select the cheapest option. Cheap is no good if it doesn't do the job!'

'Well, you always want the higher-quality, higher-priced option, even when we don't need it!'

'Yes, that's typical of your negative attitude, Dave. It should be obvious, *even to you*, that . . .' and so the argument goes on.

When this happens, it is not much fun (except for the sadistic amongst us), and it doesn't help the decision-making process! Healthy disagreement is fine, but emotional personal attacks are not. The question is how to avoid this sort of situation developing.

The Solution

Use a flipchart or wipeclean board to redirect attention away from 'eyeball to eyeball' contact between the opposing factions!

Ask the two people individually to give you their respective views and summarize *both* views on the flipchart. To ensure that all main points of each viewpoint are recorded, do not let the other party interrupt while you are doing this. This level of control tends to slow things down and encourages the two combatants to 'engage brain before engaging mouth', rather than argue across the table.

Decide! . . . You will never have all of the information you would like

The Problem

Actually making the decision is often one of the hardest steps in decision making. Some people are prepared to take risks that may accompany decision making, others are not. One question we all ask ourselves, however, is: 'Do I have the information I need to make this decision?'

Some people want to dot every 'i' and cross every 't' before they decide anything, in order to reduce the chances of being 'wrong'. In general, this is well nigh impossible to achieve. How often do you have all the information you would like? We can rarely be certain of all the facts, and so many decisions are based on at least some assumptions – for instance, we take out pensions assuming (hoping) we will be there to collect!

Failure to decide (when a decision is needed) can be a far bigger problem than making a 'wrong' decision. An old boss of mine used to say 'In a crisis, any decision is better than no decision!' so I declare some bias here. Ask yourself how you react to indecision.

The Solution

People understandably want to make the 'right' decision but they need to accept that they are unlikely ever to have *all* the information they would like. The question should be rephrased to: 'Do I have all the *essential* information to make a reasoned decision?' Decisions are often concerned to some extent with predicting the future, and some assumptions are therefore inevitable.

If we could guarantee making all of our decisions 'right', we would be lottery millionaires! All we can hope to do is to be successful with the important ones. Since some errors are inevitable, no manager should expect perfection in decision making.

Quick decisions? . . . Check the risks

The Problem

Probably 80 per cent of the decisions that we have to make fall into the category of quick decisions. Someone asks if they can have tomorrow off or if they can borrow the computer for a couple of hours. There are people who would give each detailed consideration, but most of us usually simply react immediately to these requests and use 'gut feeling'. In other words, it seems naturally right at the time.

So what is the problem? Well, a too detailed consideration may have the same effect as indecision and the 'deadline' passes, with all of the attendant problems, while a too rapid 'gut reaction' might just be wrong and cause more problems than it solves.

What we need is an approach that is *considered but fast*.

The Solution

Quick decisions do not mean instant decisions. There is usually some thinking time, even if only a minute or two. Often the options are simple: either say 'Yes' or 'No'. In these situations, school yourself to consider two questions:

1 What are the essential criteria?

2 What are the main risks on both options?

Suppose, for example, I ask to borrow your computer this afternoon. Using this idea, you think:

- I can finish the vital report for the Board by lunch time.

- 'Yes' means I will not have access if I need it, but that is unlikely to be necessary.

- 'No' means I would possibly be seen as unhelpful.

Conclusion: Agree to the request.

You might already do something like this, but unconsciously. From now on, do it consciously.

Don't limit thinking by setting criteria too early

IDEA 7

The Problem

Everyone can be creative, but some seem to find it easier than others. People often seem to link creativity to personality traits: for example, 'creative people are always extroverts'. While introverts might be less happy than extroverts to suggest the more zany solutions in a group, we suggest that this is not the reason for apparent lack of creativity. We believe this deficiency is due to 'thinking' style.

Certain people mentally screen out ideas by considering the criteria too early. For example, 'I have this idea but the cost would probably be too high, so I won't suggest it.' Consequently a potentially useful idea has been lost. Why, you might ask, is it potentially useful if it's too expensive? After all, someone might suggest a way of reducing the cost while retaining the chief benefits. This cannot be done if the idea is never suggested!

The Solution

Do not set (or even discuss) any criteria *before* or *during* a 'brainstorming' session to generate options. The objective is quantity of ideas, not quality (at this stage).

Explain that the aim is to generate new ideas and options. Criteria are important but, to avoid limiting thinking unnecessarily, they will be discussed later.

Don't evaluate during 'brainstorming'

The Problem

Despite explaining (in Idea 4.7) that criteria will only be discussed later, you will find that some participants will still try to evaluate the ideas suggested during a 'brainstorming' session:

- 'Hold on, Jane. That idea won't be acceptable to the board.'

- 'The workshop won't be able to do that, Harry.'

- 'Oh come on, be realistic, Dave. There's not enough time for that.'

Comments like these will kill creativity stone dead very quickly. How would you feel if someone kept reacting like this to your suggestions in a 'brainstorming' meeting? The effect is particularly significant with quieter people who might also lack confidence. They have to be quite brave to suggest something in the first place. In the face of comments like this, they will simply say nothing more in that session. Even the most 'thick-skinned' among us would soon give it up as a bad job.

The Solution

Set a clear rule at the onset – *no evaluation of others' ideas (yet)*.

The number of ideas generated will be significantly reduced if this rule is not followed. Explain why this is so important and stress that the ideas *will* be evaluated, but later! You might even nominate one of the team to monitor this aspect and stop the meeting immediately if the rule is breached.

Remember that some people genuinely do not even realize that they are evaluating. With the frequent evaluator, making a light joke of it can sometimes help: 'There you go again, Fred', with a smile.

IDEA 9
Encourage zany ideas – have some fun!

The Problem

Creative (or novel) ideas are not just more of the same old thing, dressed up in new clothes. The difficulty with many so-called creative brainstorming sessions is that they are just plain boring! 'Boring' in terms of either atmosphere or of the ideas generated.

Let's look first at atmosphere. The atmosphere in some of these sessions is very serious and business-meeting-like . . . 'So do you expect us all to wear funny hats and jump on the table, then?' In short, no! . . . but the atmosphere can be made far more conducive to real creativity without going totally over the top.

Boring ideas are another facet of the problem. People seem to have a tendency to play safe and only propose tried and tested ideas that have been known to work in the past. This does not generate new ideas or ways of operating.

The Solution

Atmosphere

Try to encourage an atmosphere that is friendly, positive and enthusiastic. People will feel more relaxed and this helps the creative process. Laughter is fine as long as people are laughing *with* each other and not *at* each other. There is a big difference!

Generating creative ideas

Give the group five minutes to generate some zany ideas – anything goes! Out of maybe 20 ideas there is often one 'gem' that can be modified, but the other 19 are needed to encourage it forth in the first place.

Decide on the basis of benefits versus snags

IDEA 10

The Problem

If you ask most people how they believe they make decisions, they will usually say something like: 'I weigh up the benefits of the options, do the same with the snags, and then choose.'

If we all do that, then why do we differ so much in our choices? Have you ever sat in a decision-making meeting being unable to understand why someone was so much against an option that you wanted, or where someone was supporting an option that you would never choose? Most put this down to differing 'individual judgements'. Each person believes that their judgement is right. Individual judgements will always differ: say 'Mel Gibson' or 'Pamela Anderson' and watch reactions!

Having made a considerable effort to generate creative options, it is hard at this point to consider them *rationally*, rather than simply *positively*. How, then, to resolve this mental block?

The Solution

When weighing up benefits versus snags, people seem to err towards one side or the other. Someone with a 'pessimistic' standpoint will see the snags as more significant than the benefits, whereas the person with the 'optimistic' standpoint will see benefits as more significant than risks. Thus they will probably favour different options!

If you find yourself in this situation with someone else, try to find a mutually acceptable way of *objectively* evaluating both the benefits and the snags of the options via some form of scoring scale or a 'high, medium, low' rating. Remember, though, that the figures are only an expression of your collective judgement. This seems to work far better than an emotional argument born of frustration, especially if the people who differ are asked to explain why they are judging things as they are.

Summary

Making 'logical' decisions

- Set criteria *before* thinking about the options.
- Consider a *range* of options, including 'stay as we are'.
- Always consider the risks as well as the benefits.
- Group decisions – use a flipchart to reduce potential conflict.
- Decide! . . . you will never have all of the information you would like.
- Quick decisions? – Check the risks.

Making 'creative' decisions

- Don't limit thinking by setting criteria too early.
- Don't evaluate during 'brainstorming'.
- Encourage zany ideas – have some fun!
- Decide on the basis of benefits versus snags.

Points to remember

_____

_____

_____

_____

_____

_____

_____

5 How to communicate orally and persuade

A significant proportion of our communication and persuasion is done verbally. That is not to say that written communication is unimportant – far from it! These days, though, many organizations have a 'house style' for written communications, that is, common formats for reports, use of electronic mail, and so forth. We therefore thought it beneficial to concentrate on spoken communication in this chapter.

The objectives for this chapter

After reading this chapter, you should know and understand:

- What 'oral communication' and 'persuasion' are.
- Why they are important.
- Some principles that will help you to communicate verbally and to persuade others.

'Oral communication' and why it is important

Effective oral communication does not only mean speaking clearly and concisely. It also means ensuring that information is *passed to* and *understood by the recipient*. Many people speak clearly, yet communication so often fails because what is said is either incorrectly heard or is not properly understood. Managers have to 'get things done through others', and in order for this to happen, everyone must understand what is required – that is, they must be on the same wavelength.

'Persuasion' and why it is important

We define 'persuasion' as the ability to get other people to do what you need, willingly if possible, but certainly without resorting to coercion. 'Persuasion' by fear is not persuasion, in our opinion.

The ability to persuade is vital in order to meet objectives. The days when all instructions from the boss were accepted without question are gone. People want, and expect, more involvement than that. The successful manager needs to be able to persuade in all three directions: own boss, own team, and colleagues.

Listening is active, *not* *passive*

The Problem

We all like to believe that we are good listeners. If that were true, there would be far fewer errors than there are in reality. How often do you encounter situations in which the correct message has not been received? For example, in conversation with someone you are asked to do something. Later, it transpires that you have done something different from what was required. Where does the responsibility for this misunderstanding lie?

Certainly the 'transmitter' must be clear, but the 'receiver' also has a part to play in the communication process. Have you ever come out from a meeting and a colleague says, 'I didn't understand a word of what so-and-so was saying', to which you reply, 'Well, why didn't you ask, then?' and your colleague answers, 'I didn't want to look stupid'? Too many people see 'listening' as keeping quiet and trying to concentrate on what is said and, what is more, view that as the safer option. How, then, *can* we listen better *and* deal with the 'embarrassment' factor?

The Solution

We *share* the responsibility for communication, so listening has to be an *active* process – that is, we must become involved!

The solution has two facets: listening better, and coping with embarrassment.

> 1 To listen more effectively, ensure that you have understood the main point(s) by reflecting them back to the 'transmitter'. For example, 'Did you say that the

meeting was moved to 3 p.m., Marion?' This helps you to check that you have understood the message correctly.

2 Some people wrongly think they will 'look stupid' if they do this. Actually, the reverse applies, provided it is not overdone. The 'transmitter' generally sees it as showing interest and trying to understand.

Summarize and encourage questions – it is important!

IDEA 2

The Problem

Called upon to chair meetings, most people seem to learn very quickly that occasional summaries are important for clarity and understanding. Unfortunately, this skill sometimes doesn't find its way into day-to-day communications. All too often, people try to impart extremely complex information without any summary of main points or opportunity for questions. Because *they* understand it, they assume that everyone else will! The 'receiver' can easily be made to feel as if everything is being done at full gallop when they would much prefer to trot. Interestingly, these high-speed communications often end with a question such as 'You understand all that, don't you, John?' What is John *likely* to reply? Few would have the courage to say: 'In fact you went so fast that I totally lost you after the first sentence. Would you give me an instant replay of the entire conversation please?'

The Solution

The more complex the information, the more summaries you should make. Try to break the information down into 'chunks' and summarize the main points – those points that must be understood and retained – at the end of each section. For example, a parent might spend five minutes or more explaining to their child how to cross the road safely, but they often summarize with: 'Remember, *always* look both ways before you step off the kerb!'

You should also *encourage* questions, which help understanding. Some people, however, need encouragement (not just a prompt) to ask questions. For example, 'I've covered a lot of ground here. Indeed I found it all rather confusing myself at first, so I would be surprised if there weren't a few questions in your mind. What do you think?'

IDEA 3

Use questions to deal with verbal aggression

The Problem

We define oral aggression as 'using personal attacks'. For example, 'That's typical. Fine manager you are. Mugs like me have to work on Saturday whilst you're off watching football. Paid twice my salary and no thought for anyone else but yourself, have you?' Handling this aggressive behaviour is hard! Some people seem to cope with it better than others, but no one finds it easy.

Think for a minute about how you might respond to aggressive behaviour such as this. Typical responses might include:

- 'Don't be negative. Occasional weekend work is in your contract, if you bothered to look. This *is* the time for it – and by the way, your merit rise *was* due next month!'

- 'Right . . . Well, I suppose I had better find someone else to do it then.'

The first type of response turns it into a full-blown row, and nobody wins those. Even if you (the manager) are 'right', you have dropped to the other person's emotional level. Vengeance is a powerful motive!

The second response will probably remove most, if not all, of the aggression. But what have you taught the aggressor? That bullying works! 'If I shout loudly enough, I'll win.' Note, though, that we are not saying you should *never* give in. There are some people who rarely become angry, and when they do, they are usually justified. If we make a mistake or unwittingly do something that makes someone justifiably angry, of course we should give in.

The Solution

When someone launches a personal attack at you, try asking questions.

Questions have the effect of making the person *think*, when what they really want to do is just *react*. If you can ignore the attacks and *persist* with open questions, the heat will usually subside.

Watch out for 'machine-gun' questions

The Problem

'Machine-gun' questions are a quick-fire series of questions that follow each other without a noticeable pause. For example, 'Carlos, what has caused the delay with that project? Is it too much staff absence? What do you think we can do about it? Shall I authorize some overtime?' and so on. Poor old Carlos hasn't a chance either to think or to answer. Often he is left feeling 'Which question do you want me to answer?' The 'easy' solution for most people is to answer the *last* question!

From our experience of running communications skills training, this is a common problem and people who ask 'machine-gun' questions often do not realize they are doing it. Essentially, the questioner is trying to help, but is simply being too impatient to wait for an answer. Often in these circumstances a good open question to collect information is immediately followed by one that suggests the answer.

If you are unsure whether you do this, try asking someone whose opinion you trust for their view.

The Solution

Ask questions *one at a time*, and *pause after each one* (try counting slowly to three).

This tack avoids the confusion that machine-gun questions cause, gives the responder a little time to think, and enables the situation to be handled one step at a time. The process might take longer, but the eventual outcome is far more effective and satisfactory.

Don't confuse consensus decision making with persuasion

The Problem

Most managers are involved in decision making with others. Sometimes the objective is to reach a decision in circumstances where no one favours any particular option at the outset and everyone is collectively trying to find the best solution (consensus decision making). On other occasions, the manager has a strong view about one of the options and wants to convince the others to take, or reject, this course of action (persuasion).

Unfortunately, it is all too easy to confuse the two approaches, or not even to consider them as separate. Such confusion can result in a less-than-effective solution being chosen (to keep people happy) because someone simply 'went along with it' rather than trying to persuade. Conversely, if one person is trying to persuade in a situation where all of the others feel that an impartial (objective) analysis of all options is called for, the 'persuader' may well be seen as unreasonably 'dominating'.

The Solution

Prior to any decision-making meeting (two or more people), decide what role you need to play. If you (and the others involved) have no particular objective except to find an appropriate solution, then it is 'consensus'. The aim is to hear all views and collectively choose a solution or option that everyone can 'live with'.

If, however, you feel that a particular solution or option should be adopted or rejected, then you need to be in 'persuasion' mode. So prepare your case thoroughly before the meeting: emphasize the benefits of your proposal and anticipate likely objections to it.

Know the specific result you want before trying to persuade

The Problem

This idea may appear to some to be stating the obvious. We agree! Yet you might be surprised to learn how many people do *not* have a *clear* result in mind at the onset. They have a result in mind certainly, but it is often far from clear.

An example might help. Suppose a manager needs some additional staff for a short period to complete an important project on time. He or she makes this request to their manager, and they are given two people for a week (which helps). At the end of that week, however, they go back again asking for further help because the work is still not finished. What they needed in the first place (if they had done their homework properly) was three people for a fortnight.

Some people are not specific enough in their requests. Not surprisingly, therefore, they end up with something different from what they actually need. For example:

Dad (to sixteen-year-old daughter): 'You can go to that party, but don't be back too late.'
Dad (next morning): 'I said "Not too late". It was 1 a.m. when you got back. No more parties for you!'
Daughter: 'That wasn't late! Some people were just *arriving*. I felt stupid leaving!'

This sort of difficulty happens all of the time (at work as well as at home) and is caused by people not saying specifically what they want!

The Solution

Before trying to persuade, decide the specific result that you want and don't be afraid to communicate it to the other party. Without doing this, you are likely to end up with a different result from the one you want, since the other person probably can't mind-read!

Set limits (a band) when persuading or negotiating

IDEA 7

The Problem

The problem here is, in a sense, the reverse of the problem covered in Idea 5.6 (Knowing the specific result you want). There are people who set a very specific result and then adopt an all-or-nothing approach when trying to persuade. For example:

Man (to bank manager): 'I need an overdraft of £1000 for two months.'
Bank manager: 'I can let you have £1000 for one month.'
Man: 'It's two months, or nothing!'
Bank manager: 'Right. It's nothing then!'

Didn't that work well!

Negotiation is often – not always, but often – an integral part of persuasion. Room to manoeuvre is important. Some people, though, never allow themselves that room and end up in a situation similar to the man above – paying a price for inflexibility.

The Solution

Effective persuaders and negotiators set limits – usually a band within which they are prepared to operate. This band is set by a series of questions, such as:

- What is the best I can *realistically* hope to achieve? (£1000 for two months)

- What would I be happy to achieve? (£1000 for one month)
- What is the lower (or upper) limit, beyond which I cannot go? (£750 for one month)

Note 'realistically' in the first question. Going in with a totally unrealistic 'demand' will generate animosity right from the start because the other person knows they stand no chance of closing the gap. Be honest with yourself about what can be achieved.

Treat 'bottom-line' people differently from 'detail' people

The Problem

When trying to persuade, giving either too much or too little information can cause severe problems.

Have you ever heard a person interrupt in the middle of a presentation and say, 'Just give me the bottom line!' In effect, they are saying: 'I don't need all this detail in order to respond at this stage.' It may be impatience, but it could also be a compliment: 'I know you have already done your homework, so give me the proposal.' This is a 'bottom-line' person in action.

Conversely, the presenter might be covering the main points only and be constantly interrupted with questions such as 'How exactly did you arrive at that figure?' or 'What risks have you considered?' It may be distrust, but is often caused by the questioner's need to verify that the i's have been dotted and the t's crossed to their satisfaction. This is a 'detail' person in action.

The mistake is in not responding to the needs of the person you are trying to persuade, and, as a result, failing to persuade.

The Solution

Always prepare thoroughly, irrespective of how much information you intend to impart. Decide whether you are dealing with a 'bottom-line' person or a 'detail' person and act accordingly. Remember that some people act differently depending on the situation.

- *The 'bottom-line' person* – Give them your proposal right at the start along with the chief benefits. Then ask them if they need further information and respond if they do. (That is why it is so important to prepare thoroughly.)

- *The 'detail' person* – Explain the process you have used to arrive at a proposal and ask which areas they would like you to cover in detail. Be prepared only to give a summary if that is all they want.

A win/win approach is better than win/lose

IDEA 9

The Problem

Persuasion (and negotiation) is seen by some as a form of competitive sport: 'I need to win this one, and if that means beating the opposition into submission, so be it!'

These people have the mistaken impression that, in order to win, their 'opponent(s)' must lose. That is simply not true! The main difficulty with this approach is the aftermath: that is, you might win the battle but lose the war, because of the bad feeling your action has generated. Some folk will not accept the biblical quotation: 'Vengeance is mine; I will repay, saith the Lord.' They prefer to do a little 'repaying' of their own when the opportunity presents itself sooner or later – sometimes *much* later.

The Solution

Use a win/win approach: that is, you endeavour to ensure that both parties gain something. We see it as a form of 'horse-trading'. You might just try for the bigger/faster/cheaper horse, but, in the end, the other party still receives some reward. Nothing is gained if you shoot your opponent's horse!

Win/win means that both parties leave the discussion feeling that they have gained something from it. One might gain more than the other, but there is still gain on both sides.

IDEA 10 *Provide a 'doorway'*

The Problem

This idea links with 'win/win' in Idea 5.9. Occasionally you may find yourself in a straightforward situation that demands a 'yes' or 'no', or a 'do it' or 'don't do it' outcome. In cases like this you might ask, 'Well, how can I bring about a win/win result here?' He or she either accepts your decision or not. There is no room for any form of compromise.

The outcome may have to be a firm decision one way or the other, but that should not mean that one person must lose absolutely everything. Our own egos are very important to us. If we are seen by others to have failed totally, we don't usually feel great about ourselves at that point.

The problem, then, is how do you adopt a win/win approach in a straightforward decision situation without compromising your own position and objectives.

The Solution

We were given the following very good tip many years ago that helps: 'Never push people into a corner without providing a doorway.'

The 'doorway' is there to allow people to save face when they have 'lost' in this type of straightforward situation. Some examples of these 'doorways' might include:

- Enabling them to gain something unrelated to the issue under discussion.

- Offering support by explaining an unpopular decision to the team.

- Accepting a proposal from them that would prevent a similar unpopular decision in the future.

Try to consider what possible 'doorways' might exist *before* you meet.

IDEA 11
Honesty is usually the best policy.

The Problem

Let's be kind. Some people 'modify the truth' when trying to persuade (and even when communicating generally). They seem to have little trust in people and then wonder why *they* are accorded so little trust and respect themselves.

We asked 70 people from different organizations which personal characteristics they looked for in a manager. Ninety per cent placed 'Inspires respect and trust' in the top five (out of fifteen) characteristics. Would anyone earn respect and trust without honesty?

'Modifying the truth' might win the first skirmish but ultimately it will lose you the campaign. Sooner or later, someone will find out the truth. Then, what price trust and respect in future dealings?

The Solution

'Honesty' does not mean telling everyone everything – but it means that what you *do* say is the truth. Sometimes confidential information cannot be imparted, but you can often explain why you cannot discuss it.

When trying to persuade, tell people what you want. Some would-be persuaders don't do this as they mistakenly think that they may gain more by being vague. This is rarely the case!

It isn't helpful to tell someone that what they have done is fine when it is not, and then complain about them to someone else. It *is* possible to be honest, yet tactful. If you have a concern, don't ignore it – tell them how you feel. Tell the truth but protect their feelings.

Summary

How to communicate orally

- Listening is *active*, not passive.
- Summarize and encourage questions – it is important!
- Use questions to deal with oral aggression.
- Watch out for 'machine-gun' questions.
- Don't confuse consensus decision making with persuasion.

How to persuade

- Know the specific result you want before trying to persuade.
- Set limits (a band) when persuading or negotiating.
- Treat 'bottom-line' people differently from 'detail' people.
- A win/win approach is better than win/lose.
- Provide a 'doorway'.
- Honesty is usually the best policy.

Points to remember

_____

_____

_____

_____

_____

_____

6 How to encourage your team to achieve the results you need

Encouraging your team to achieve the results needed is no easy task for any manager, experienced or otherwise. The approaches that can be used to encourage vary enormously, person to person and situation to situation.

While there are no easy answers to this task, there are some basic guidelines, and we hope that the ideas in this chapter might just help. Encouraging your team to achieve results involves both leadership and motivation, which often run alongside each other: that is, we often lead and motivate simultaneously. For convenience in this chapter, we have separated the ideas relating to the two skills.

The objectives for this chapter

After reading this chapter, you should know and understand:

● What 'leadership' and 'motivation' mean.

● Why they are important and interlinked.

● Some principles that will help you to lead and motivate.

'Leadership' and why it is important

We define leadership as 'knowing what is required and using the right approach to enable the team to gain its objective'. By 'right approach' we mean appropriate for both the circumstances and the people involved. We are sure that you can think of instances where a manager used the wrong approach, and paid the price for it! However, the right approach in leadership can yield amazing results. Everyone is different and each person will probably approach a given situation in a slightly different way – and that is as it should be. The ideas on 'leadership' in this chapter will not change you as a person, but will suggest some principles for you to consider.

'Motivation' and why it is important

Motivation is a word we all use often. Yet if you ask twenty people to define motivation, you are likely to receive twenty different answers – not wrong, just different. Some people feel that the only true motivation is self-motivation. Certainly some inspiration, some desire to succeed, may well have to come from within, but that does not mean that a manager cannot help! We therefore define motivation as 'encouraging someone to give their best willingly'.

While not always the case, there does seem to be a correlation between motivation and results. A motivated person usually achieves results or, put another way, achievement usually motivates.

Know where you are going

The Problem

Some managers seem to view leadership as simply providing day-to-day direction for the team and dealing with the everyday problems that arise. While this aspect is important, it does tend to make life rather static, and the emphasis swings towards maintaining the status quo. As a result, nothing changes, moves forward or improves.

A manager of an accounts department (with an enormous outstanding debt from invoices owing for over 120 days) was once heard to remark to a director: 'Well, we do receive the money invoiced eventually, don't we?' The director's reply was fairly predictable: 'True, but shouldn't you be looking at ways of ensuring quicker payment of our invoices? Otherwise there may possibly not be enough in the bank to pay your salary next month!'

The Solution

The best leaders seem to us to have certain things in common. One common factor is that they all have a clear vision of the future which is different from the present, and represents an improvement.

Consider the following possibilities:

- Look at your principal objectives and ask yourself if they do, or *should*, represent an improvement over where you are now.

- How about that good idea you have had sitting in the back of your mind, but so far have done nothing with? Try turning it into an objective for yourself and your team.

- Ask yourself (and your team): 'What should the department be doing in one or two years' time, and what should we be doing *now* to get there?'

Don't ask for 'commitment' when all you can reasonably expect is 'acceptance'

The Problem

We define 'commitment' as 'I want to do it', whereas 'acceptance' is 'I have to do it'.

Some managers seem to set themselves the unreasonable target of gaining commitment from their people on *everything*!

Have you ever sat through a one-and-a-half hour meeting at which you were asked for your views on some issue, only to be told at the end that 'the board' had already made the decision? Irritating, isn't it? The manager wanted to *appear* democratic but in reality needed to be more autocratic than he or she would usually be.

The Solution

Consider the circumstances you are facing and ask yourself whether you require commitment or just acceptance from your people.

Some decisions a manager has to make are bound to be unpopular. Suppose the board decides that, in order to save money and jobs, it is necessary for everyone with a company car to downgrade it on the next change. Probably nobody is going to welcome that idea, and the likelihood of gaining commitment is zero! Acceptance, though, is feasible if the situation is properly explained and the reasons given – but don't expect people to like it!

The reverse of course is also true. Mere 'acceptance' is unacceptable if what you need is true 'commitment'.

Don't settle for 'acceptance' when you really need 'commitment'

The Problem

In Idea 6.2, we defined 'commitment' as 'I want to do it' and 'acceptance' as 'I have to do it'.

Being content with simple acceptance when *commitment is needed* is dangerous, to say the least. 'Acceptance' means that the person feels he or she has no choice except to do whatever is required, but is likely to do only the minimum that is absolutely necessary.

A salesperson was *told* to sell five products on behalf of another sales team to enable them to meet their monthly target. He sold the five required *and no more*, even though the opportunity to sell more was there if he had taken it . . . and he knew it! Had his manager originally asked for commitment, as he should have done, this situation might not have arisen – but then the manager never did find out about the ignored opportunity.

The Solution

'Commitment' usually – but not inevitably – equals involvement!

Commitment through involvement means asking for the person's views and feelings and being prepared *genuinely* to discuss them in order to arrive at a suitable outcome.

Make sure that you separate 'open' from 'closed' questions here. Open questions net information and are more useful, whereas closed questions just produce 'Yes/No' answers. For example:

- How do you think we should tackle it? (Open question)

- You will do that, won't you? (Closed question)

Commitment without much involvement may well be possible if the person sees you as the expert in that situation and is happy to trust your judgement.

Don't be afraid to say 'I don't know'

4

The Problem

When first promoted to a management job, people are usually very aware of the need to earn the respect of the team they now manage. They believe that, as manager, they should have all the answers that the team needs in order to do its various jobs effectively, otherwise the team will not respect them in their new role. They think that if they say they don't know, they will lose credibility.

Often, this fear of admitting we don't know causes even more significant difficulties. The sort of problems that can be generated are as follows:

- The manager might guess (incorrectly and without admitting it) at an answer, with the result that the team believes the information to be true when it is not, and the team's subsequent actions are consequently also wrong.

- The manager waffles, the team recognizes it as waffle, and the manager's credibility suffers.

- Because of inadequate background information, the manager makes inappropriate decisions about possible actions.

The Solution

As a rule of thumb, it seems to take three to six months for the new manager to realize that the team does *not* expect him or her to have all the answers.

There is no loss of credibility in *occasionally* saying:

- 'I don't know, but I will find out!' or
- 'I'm not sure which is the best way to proceed. What do you think?'

In fact, our contention is that this approach *increases* credibility rather than diminishes it, provided it is not being done all of the time.

Don't respond negatively when challenged

IDEA 5

The Problem

Unfortunately, some managers appear to treat *any* form of disagreement as some form of personal insult, considering it to show a lack of respect or a challenge to their authority. To use the comedian's phrase, 'They are sad people!'

Often the person who is 'disagreeing' is in turn attacked by the manager. For example: 'Don't question my decisions, Jane. I have made the decision. Your job is simply to *do* it!' Not surprisingly, this kind of rebuke often has damaging consequences for that individual's motivation.

Few of us enjoy a negative reaction to our ideas. The problem is that managers sometimes fail to look at the *nature* of the 'disagreement'. Consider these three negative reactions:

1 'I am concerned that there won't be time to do that by the deadline.'

2 'It won't work – we tried that before.'

3 'Sometimes you think you only have to speak and everyone else has to jump five feet in the air. You can't insist that I work at the weekend'.

Some people would respond equally strongly to all three statements, because they are all negative! In other words, they are not differentiating between them! But before reading any further, try deciding how you should react to each.

The Solution

1 This statement gives the reason for disagreement and is indicating a valid problem. You should treat it constructively and find a solution or compromise together.

2 No reason is given in this statement. You should therefore concentrate on finding the reason and, if possible, elicit a solution from the individual.

3 This statement is a personal attack. Try not to hit back, for that response will gain nothing. Cool the situation down by asking the person to explain why they feel as they do. Only when they have cooled down, should you try to deal with their reasons. Remember, they may have a point, albeit badly put, and perhaps you were wrong!

Avoid the 'provide goodies' trap

IDEA 6

The Problem

So what is the 'provide goodies' trap? Perhaps an example might best illustrate what we mean.

If there is a tough or unpopular job to be done, some managers think that, in order for it to be done, they must resort to some motivational 'managerial bribery'. Thus, for example, they might say: 'Carlos, I know you will need to work late this week to meet this new deadline. But if you do it, then you can take your partner out for a meal at the company's expense at the weekend'.

At first glance, you might think: 'What on earth is wrong with that? At least the manager is showing appreciation.' Some team members may well see it that way, but others might see it as 'bribery', and could even be offended by it. Secondly, what is Carlos likely to expect if asked to work late in future?

What should we do, therefore, if we cannot use bribery?

The Solution

Use 'recognition': that is, show your thanks and appreciation *after the event*. Material rewards are not always necessary. People don't usually do things for material rewards alone . . . have you never done anything simply to help other people? Often a sincere 'Thanks for what you did' is sufficient when well put.

If you do feel that some action beyond the call of duty warrants a more tangible form of recognition for the person concerned, consider springing it as a surprise afterwards, and only ever do so when it is genuinely warranted. Let such reward become the norm and thereafter it will be expected by all and sundry.

From our research, we know that recognition is a very powerful motivator. 'Bribery', however, might just offend and consequently could actually be counterproductive.

IDEA 7 Be prepared to make a decision

The Problem

There is an alternative phrase for being prepared, as a manager, to take the responsibility for actually *making* decisions: it is called 'doing the job you are paid for'!

Note the stress on 'making'. Often, actually analysing the pros and cons of the various options is not too difficult – saying 'We will decide on that one' is the hard task. Unfortunately, some managers seem to make a career out of being indecisive, that is, 'sitting on the fence'. Whenever they are asked for a decision, they ask for more information, or say that they need to think about it, or just do nothing. For a team member who does not have the necessary authority to decide, this is one of the most frustrating situations imaginable, as you will certainly know if you have experienced it.

'Marion, you need to decide if XYZ Ltd can have 20 per cent discount on this order for £2 million by five o'clock today, otherwise they are likely to buy elsewhere.' 'Leave it with me, John. I'll have a think about it', and off goes Marion to a meeting.

Five o'clock comes and . . . nothing! Next day John checks with XYZ – the order is lost! Why? Failure to make a decision when it was needed.

The Solution

Consider the consequences of *not* deciding (see Idea 4.5) and the effect on the motivation of the team member concerned.

If you honestly do need time to weigh up the facts, find out if there is any deadline for decision and explain why you need some time. And make sure that you *do* respond in time.

You might also like to consider whether it is appropriate to delegate authority (with limits) to the team member for future decisions of this type. If that course of action is feasible, time may be saved by everyone (and motivation increased as well).

Ask 'What do you enjoy doing?' rather than 'What motivates you?'

The Problem

Most managers accept that motivation is important and some actually try to find out what motivates their people! That's an obvious thing to do, say the sceptics. *No, it is not.* In fact, what many managers do is make *assumptions* about what they believe motivates their team members. These assumptions are often based on the manager's own values, which may not of course be those of the individual concerned.

A common false assumption is that: 'Everyone must want promotion, therefore something which will help them to develop along this route will motivate.' Wrong! Not everyone does want the responsibility that goes with promotion, and pushing extra responsibility at them might well demotivate.

Going a stage further, some managers realize the danger of assumptions and therefore ask: 'What motivates you then, Anton?' Now this is a very hard and complex question to answer, and, not surprisingly, people tend to give simple off-the-cuff answers: 'I could do with more money', or 'A new car would be acceptable'. In the first place, however, few managers would be able to provide more cash or a new car. Secondly, are such rewards the real answer to long-term motivation anyway? How long will the effects of a cash increase or new car last?

The Solution

Try asking, 'What do you *enjoy doing*, Anton?' – and don't worry about the pause that will follow your question, as Anton thinks this one through.

Anton's answers are in point of fact likely to give you a far better indication of what actually motivates that individual than either of the approaches mentioned previously. You can then plan together how in future you might use some or all of the factors revealed in the answers.

Genuine praise is a powerful motivator

The Problem

We believe that there is a current philosophy in business that underlies the actions of some managers, as follows: 'If you are doing something wrong, I will talk to you about it. If things are going well, I will leave you alone.' Consequently, team members may warn new members joining the team: 'Don't expect any thanks from him, but if you make a mistake, you will soon know about it!'

Unfortunately, some managers who adopt this philosophy don't even realize they are doing so, but members of their team certainly recognize it! Other managers who do recognize it are concerned that praise will be seen as idle flattery and have little effect (or even a negative one).

The problems associated with this approach are twofold:

- First, any time the manager calls someone into the office to talk, that team member's shoulders immediately slump. 'What have I done wrong now?' is the initial reaction.

- Second, everyone has strengths as well as weaknesses, but this approach misses the opportunity to reinforce the strengths. In consequence, those strengths may even decay in the struggle to correct weaknesses.

The Solution

It is as important for a manager to praise work done well as it is for him or her to correct matters when things are not done properly.

Most people want objective, balanced feedback from their manager, and genuine praise is an important part of that. 'Praise' to us means recognition backed up by hard fact. For example: 'I thought your meeting went very well. The objectives were clear to all. You turned Mike's disagreements into something positive, and all of our objectives for it were met. Well done! What did you learn from running it?'

Don't expect everybody to be highly motivated

IDEA 10

The Problem

Would you class yourself as 'highly motivated'? Think for a minute about why you feel as you do. Perhaps the job, the people you work with, and/or the organization provide something that is important to you. From our experience in running courses for over twenty years, most managers (or aspiring managers) believe that they are well motivated, otherwise they would not be effective in their jobs. There are exceptions, but not many!

If a manager is motivated and giving their best most of the time, the danger is that they understandably expect everyone in their team to do likewise. They cannot understand why some people do not seem to respond to a set of circumstances in the way that they themselves respond. They try everything they can think of to create a positive reaction, or at least some slight show of enthusiasm, but without success. While their intention is laudable, they are (probably) expecting the impossible.

The Solution

As we have said before, don't make assumptions. Check first how people feel. Accept that some people will never be as highly motivated as you. They are happy to do the job adequately for which they are paid, go home, and forget about it! If they are content doing that, who is to say that anything is wrong? Not everyone wants extra responsibility, promotion and so on. In fact, there would not be sufficient opportunities if they did.

Put your motivational effort into those who *will* respond, and maintain the current motivational level of those who can't or don't wish to go further in the inspirational stakes.

Some managers may see this approach as defeatist. We feel that it is realistic!

Summary

Leadership

- Know where you are going.
- Don't ask for 'commitment' when all you can reasonably expect is 'acceptance'.
- Don't settle for 'acceptance' when you really need 'commitment'.
- Don't be afraid to say 'I don't know'.
- Don't respond negatively when challenged.

Motivation

- Avoid the 'provide goodies' trap.
- Be prepared to *make* a decision.
- Ask 'What do you enjoy doing?' rather than 'What motivates you?'
- Genuine praise is a powerful motivator.
- Don't expect everybody to be highly motivated.

Points to remember

_____

_____

_____

_____

_____

_____

7 How to delegate

Delegation is probably one of the hardest skills for a manager to learn. The uppermost feeling is often: 'If I delegate, things will be out of my control. I don't want a failure, so I'll do it myself.' This results in a closed loop, and an overburdened manager!

The main barrier to delegation is therefore that of 'fear'. Yet good – that is, effective – delegation means that the task is *under* control, not *out of* control.

The objectives for this chapter

After reading this chapter, you should know and understand:

- What 'delegation' is.
- Why it is so important.
- Some principles that will help you to delegate effectively.

'Delegation'

We define delegation as: 'entrusting part of your job as a manager to (usually) a direct report, together with the responsibility and authority necessary for carrying it out'.

Responsibility and authority can be delegated, but account-ability – that is, being ultimately answerable for the activity – cannot.

The act of delegation must be separated from simply issuing work. Issuing work means deciding which member of the team should carry out some task that is part of their normal role anyway. 'Delegation', on the other hand, involves giving someone a task that is normally part of the manager's job.

Why delegation is important

There are several reasons. Good – that is, effective – delegation is important for the following reasons:

- It enables the manager to spend more time on more important tasks.
- It is a very good way of developing people who wish to advance in the organization.
- It is highly motivational – although, if done badly, the reverse is also true!

Pick the right task

The Problem

First, some managers believe they are 'delegating' when in fact all they are doing is to issue work that would normally be done by a member of the team anyway.

Secondly, there are those who do actually consider delegating part of their job, but then the only tasks that seem to be delegated are those which the manager can't be bothered to do personally.

Thirdly, some managers only delegate when they are in 'work-overload': 'Mavis, would you finish off the figures on my monthly report for me. I have to go to that section meeting straight away and I won't have time to do them.'

The crux of the problem is which tasks to delegate.

The Solution

Make an initial list of all the main tasks you perform. Then ask yourself which of these tasks would be worth delegating for the following reasons:

- It would save you valuable time.

- It might motivate a member of the team.

- It would help to develop someone's skills and/or knowledge.

- It causes others problems when you are not around to do it personally.

- You enjoy doing it and therefore hang on to it possessively (honesty is required here)!

Now that you have identified those tasks which you *could* delegate, the next idea examines the choice of the right person to delegate to.

Pick the right person

The Problem

We would wager that there is at least one member of your team whom you would immediately consider as a prime candidate for a delegated task. Often they are quite experienced and so need little briefing from you, and will always offer to help in a crisis. Every manager needs – or would like, did you say? – someone like that in their team. The danger is that such a person will take on too much. Overload a willing horse and its legs are likely to collapse!

There is another facet to the problem. Some managers never even consider delegating anything to an inexperienced or new member of the team because they *assume*, perhaps subconsciously, that no experience means no ability.

How, then, do you go about choosing the right person for the task?

The Solution

First, ask yourself why you are considering delegating this particular task. Now think about the skill and knowledge requirements of the task, and the individual strengths and needs of the people in your team in this particular field (previous discussion at appraisal or review meetings should help you here).

Next, try to match the task requirements to the individual strengths and needs. Remember, do not assume that no experience means no ability – check!

Now that you have decided *who* is the right person to do the job, set a specific objective: for example, develop Andrew's financial control skills and knowledge within three months by delegating production of the monthly 'budget versus spend' report to him.

Challenge, but avoid it being seen as an impossibility

The Problem

Karen (the manager): 'Hello, Dawn. Come on in and have a seat. I have just been told that I am going on a management course next week and I need your help. You know, we must obtain some more personal computers – one just isn't enough for us now. Next week I was going to put together a proposal to justify their purchase and discuss it with our director. As I am away now and you're my number two, I think you should have a crack at it.'

Dawn (the deputy): 'I realize our need, Karen, but I have never put a proposal together; much less tried to persuade a director with one! I'm not at all sure that I could do that at the moment. I have no idea how to prepare a presentation, let alone give one.'

Karen: 'Everyone has to start somewhere. I had to do that sort of thing when I was in your position 18 months ago. Our old manager used to believe in throwing people in at the deep end, and that's how I learned. This will be a good challenge for you. There's nothing like a meeting with a director to focus the mind. I'm sure you'll cope if you give it a try.'

Dawn: 'Well, I sincerely doubt it . . . and you won't even be here to help.'

How do you think that Dawn would fare? What is seen by Karen as a 'challenge' is seen by Dawn as 'impossible'! This mismatch between the manager's perception and that of the team member seems to be a recurring problem in business.

The Solution

Because *you* can do something (or could when you were in their job) does not mean that *they* can necessarily do it! Before deciding to delegate a task to a particular team member, ask yourself if they have (or can develop, in the time available) the knowledge and/or skills, as well as the confidence, to cope with the task. If they genuinely see it as impossible, they are unlikely to succeed.

Trust people – give them the authority they need

IDEA 4

The Problem

To quote Robert Townsend: 'All decisions should be made as low as possible in the organisation. The Charge of the Light Brigade was ordered by an officer who wasn't there looking at the territory.' (*Up the Organisation*, 1970.)

Some managers seem altogether too happy to delegate responsibility to team members but never give them the authority they need to do the job properly. In this context we define 'authority' as the power to make independent decisions. As we discussed in the introduction to this chapter, failure to delegate effectively probably stems from fear. However, there can be little that is more frustrating for a team member than to feel that they have to keep running back to the manager every time a decision on even the most minor aspects of a delegated job is needed.

The problem? How do you delegate the authority without relinquishing control or abdicating responsibility altogether?

The Solution

Delegate authority to the team member for making independent decisions *within set limits*. This should protect you from serious disasters.

For example, suppose that you delegate, to one of your people, the task of negotiating with a customer a price for an important product. He or she will probably ask, 'How far can I go?' to which you would reply along the following lines: 'We have quoted £80,000 for one module. Now they find they need two and therefore want to negotiate. You can negotiate a discount of up to 10 per cent – that gives a minimum price of £144,000 for two modules – or a lower discount and free maintenance worth £3,000, whichever you think most appropriate at the time. If they insist on a deal that would take us below the minimum price of £144,000, check with me before agreeing to anything.'

Don't try to 'dress up' boring tasks as something special

The Problem

What might be *said*: 'Can you spare a minute, Andrea? Something very important has cropped up and I think you will be interested. The board want an analysis of our sales over the last year by product and by geographical district. As my deputy, you will have to prepare analyses one day, so why not start now?'

Sounds fine so far but . . .

What is actually *meant*: 'Andrea, I'm strapped for time and our director is screaming for information. For the next couple of hours, I'll call you figures and you just punch the calculator and feed me the answers. By the way, I haven't the time to actually *explain* any of it at the moment!'

Incredibly, there are quite a few managers who not only make a habit of this sort of approach, but, even worse, also delude themselves that their 'victim' actually *believes* what they tell them! Of course, it doesn't take many occurrences for the 'deputy', or whoever their victim happens to be, to work out what is going on. Thus, when the manager says he or she has 'an interesting job' for them, they immediately associate it with a boring or mundane task, because that's what past experience of this manager has taught them.

The Solution

If you need a pair of arms or legs to help with some boring but necessary task, *be honest!*

Provided that, on other occasions, you do try to delegate interesting and challenging tasks, most team members would be prepared to help out with the routine work. But don't try to deceive them – it doesn't work!

Don't make assumptions for people – encourage them to do the planning!

The Problem

There is a genuine belief among some managers that delegation involves telling team members what is required, exactly how it should be carried out, and by when. When asked why they do this, two interesting reasons are frequently put forward:

1 'Well, I have done the job umpteen times before and so I know the best way.'

2 'They haven't done it before, so they wouldn't know how to.'

Have you spotted the two (possibly incorrect) assumptions that have been made?

1 Because someone has carried out a task many times, it does not necessarily follow that they know the best, or indeed the only, way of doing it.

2 Because someone has not done the job before, it does not *necessarily* follow that they cannot broadly understand what is needed, or how to do it, or even how long it might take. Sometimes these so-called uninformed people just might, if given the chance, come up with a new method that is even more effective than that used for months or even years in the past.

The Solution

Whatever the task, some sort of plan is needed (even if fairly brief) to show who needs to do what and by when. Rather than suggest the plan personally, try asking your team members how *they* would tackle the task. Then ask yourself whether their method would achieve the objective. If it will work (even though it may differ from your approach), let them do it their way, for they will be more committed to *their* plan. Provide advice only if a basic flaw appears in their plan or if they have no idea how to go about the task.

Encourage people to suggest checkpoints and give them access to you

IDEA
7

The Problem

When considering whether to delegate some task or other, a common fear that seems to haunt many managers is the apparent 'loss of control': that is, 'If I delegate this task, I'm not doing it, so I'm not in control of it.' Attempting to overcome this difficulty, as he or she sees it, the manager sets up frequent review dates to meet and 'see how things are going', and then wonders why the team member does not show up for (at least some of) these meetings. The manager now starts to develop 'delegator's twitch'!

Even worse is to follow. You find the manager constantly looking over the team member's shoulder, asking how things are going. How do you think the team member sees this? Helpful? Showing interest? Not a bit of it. They usually see it as *interference* or *distrust*!

The problem, then, is how to maintain some control without interfering or appearing not to trust the person to whom you have delegated the work.

The Solution

Two actions which should help are as follows:

1 Encourage them to suggest the checkpoints: that is, the stages in the task when you should meet. Probably, they will suggest the points that you would have suggested, but this is *their* plan!

2 Give them access to you if they want to discuss any aspects of the task: 'I have given you the job because I know you can do it and the last thing I want to do is interfere. If you want to discuss anything, just come and talk to me.' They now know that they can now talk to you when *they* want, and have been given the responsibility for doing so.

Accept a few minor mistakes whilst they are learning

The Problem

If, at some stage, you have learned to ride a motorbike or drive a car, think about how the learning process went: horrible crunching of gears, stalling at traffic lights, forgetting to signal occasionally, and so on. Then gradually you became proficient, more skilled, more experienced.

Delegation can be rather like learning to drive. Very few people have the knack of doing an unfamiliar job perfectly at the first attempt. In fairness, most managers realize this, and so to 'help' (as they see it), they are very specific about what they want and exactly how it must be done. There is of course sometimes a case for doing this, but if the objective is to help the person to *develop*, that individual requires room to manoeuvre, to be allowed the few mistakes that are inevitable as he or she learns.

However, some managers seem to expect 'perfection' right from the start, which takes the form of: 'Do it my way exactly so that you won't make any mistakes and let me down.' What sort of learning experience or development is that for trainees? They have been trained to be unthinking robots!

The Solution

Be prepared to accept a few *minor* mistakes while their skill and knowledge develops. At strategic points, jointly review their performance on the task to find out what they have learned and what they would do differently next time.

During the discussion when you are jointly planning the task, try to anticipate and prevent any *serious* problems (disasters!). Agree what actions are needed and, together, work out the best way of monitoring them.

At the end of your discussion, check how they feel *about doing the task*

The Problem

Over the years on training courses, we have asked many managers what should be discussed when trying to delegate. Many good points come out from these discussions but there is one area that is very rarely mentioned: how the team member *feels* about doing the task that is being delegated to him or her.

Some managers explain the task and what is involved in its successful completion at considerable length, believing that a clear explanation is all that is necessary – that is, if you fully understand it, you will be prepared to do it. Their closing remark is usually: 'Do you understand all that?' What is the team member supposed to say? The answer is likely to be a vague nod or a mumbled 'S'pose so', and the manager then believes everything is fine. The team member might well understand the task, but that does not mean that *they want to do it*.

Successful delegation requires the team member's commitment and motivation, and it is hard to see how any manager can *know* that this has been achieved unless he or she *asks* the team member. Managers generally accept this point, but most seem to rely on the mental waves, or 'vibes' coming back from the team member. While some managers are certainly good at this, the chief danger is that 'vibes' can be easily misinterpreted.

Good delegation is *not* confined to simply explaining or discussing the task!

The Solution

Do not rely only on 'vibes'. Towards the end of your discussion, ask the team member specifically how they feel about doing the task, and listen carefully to their answer! If they are not happy about the task, your instructions or their own role, then you must find out why in some detail. Finally, you and the team member must work out together a way of dealing with their concerns.

Avoid the 'black hole' – review the outcome after the task has been completed

The Problem

Most managers will have some way of monitoring progress on the delegated task as it proceeds. However, once the task has been completed, a strange phenomenon seems to rear its head – we call it 'the black hole'.

The task (an important report, say) is delegated effectively, the team member is happy to do the work, and preparation of the report proceeds on plan with regular review discussions (praise for things done well and constructive discussion about any difficulties). Eventually the report is completed successfully and left on the boss's desk. Then what? Often, absolutely nothing! The report disappears into a 'black hole' never to be seen or mentioned again.

Delegation should generally be a learning experience, and we believe that the most valuable learning comes from reviewing the outcome of a project after it has been completed. Yet, while there is feedback and discussion during the course of the project, a review discussion after the event is extremely rare. Thus a key opportunity for positive learning – and motivation for the future – has been missed.

The Solution

After completion of the task, agree with the team member a date to sit down and review how the project went. Four questions (or your own version of them) should be directed to the team member, and then discussed by you both:

1 How do you feel it went?

2 What went particularly well, and why?

3 What difficulties were there, and how were they handled?

4 What have you learned from it, and how will you use it?

This discussion probably won't take too long, but the resulting benefits will be more than worth the time spent, and it avoids the 'black hole'!

Summary

The art of good delegation

- Pick the right task.
- Pick the right person.
- Challenge, but avoid it being seen as an impossibility.
- Trust people – give them the authority they need.
- Don't try to 'dress up' boring tasks as something special.
- Don't make assumptions for people – encourage them to do the planning!
- Encourage people to suggest checkpoints and give them access to you.
- Accept a few minor mistakes whilst they are learning.
- At the end of your discussion, check how they *feel* about doing the task.
- Avoid the 'black hole' – review the outcome after the task has been completed.

Points to remember

_____

_____

_____

_____

_____

_____

8 How to present information and proposals

If there is one aspect that seems to make the adrenalin flow, it is the prospect of having to present information or make proposals to others in the organization. Even normally self-confident managers find themselves undergoing 'panic attacks' and discover they have contracted the 'What if . . . ?' syndrome, the symptoms of which condition are as follows:

- 'What if I dry up?'
- 'What if I gabble?'
- 'What if I can't answer their questions?'
- 'What if they reject my ideas?'

This chapter contains some ideas to help with this dreaded 'illness' and its symptoms.

The objectives for this chapter

After reading this chapter, you should know and understand:

- The difference between presenting information and presenting proposals.
- The importance of the effective presentation of ideas.

- Some principles that will help you to present your ideas effectively.

The difference between presenting information and presenting proposals

We define presenting information as: 'formally imparting information, opinions, and/or ideas to others so that they are not only heard but are also understood'.

Presenting proposals goes one step further by adding the element of persuasion in a formal situation (usually to a group).

Why the ability to present your ideas effectively is so important

The ability effectively to impart information to groups is vital if the message is to be listened to and understood. We have all sat through a poor presentation at some time or another, but how much of it did you actually absorb? Similarly, your recommendations will only be accepted – which is the whole point of the exercise – if you are able to present your proposal effectively.

Nerves are
1 normal

The Problem

In the introduction to this chapter we referred to the concerns that everyone has when they know they have to deliver some form of presentation. 'Nerves' affect everyone, but some people show it more than others. Typical symptoms include:

- Heart pumping
- Damp/shaking hands
- Wobbly legs
- Talking too fast
- Missing out key information
- Knot in the stomach
- Wavering voice
- Dry mouth
- Losing direction/drying up
- Fidgeting

Which of these symptoms do you suffer from?

Don't worry! There is nothing wrong with you if you do exhibit any of the symptoms, for they are all *quite natural reactions*.

The Solution

Nerves, if you suffer from them, can never be entirely eliminated, but their effect can be reduced to manageable proportions. How? By *adequate preparation*. The better your preparation, the less will nerves affect you. Make sure, therefore, that you allow adequate time to prepare.

IDEA 2

Gain their interest early

The Problem

Have you ever sat in a presentation wondering 'What is this going to cover?' or 'Why do I need to listen to this?'

A chap from a finance department spent over an hour explaining last year's results and next year's budget to a group of managers – bags of detail and 'accountant-speak'. After the presentation, most of the managers saw it as a total waste of time. Those few who had managed to stay awake for the whole hour went off delighted with the prospect of having some extra cash in their budgets next year to buy desperately needed capital equipment. The others only found out later as the requests went in.

If only the financial man had emphasized the extra cash early on, he would have had a far more attentive audience throughout his presentation. But, because he failed to gain interest at an early point, he failed to achieve his objective of informing all the people of the situation so that they could act.

There were other improvements that could have been made but we will reach those later in this chapter.

The Solution

If you want people to listen properly to you, gain their interest early!

The best way of doing this is to *give them a benefit* for listening to you. Suppose our accountant friend above had said: 'I am delighted to tell you that there is £X available next year for new capital equipment which we know you all desperately need. Before I talk about next year's budget, we must understand how everyone generated the cash this year so that we can do more of the same next year, hopefully with a similar beneficial effect.' If you were one of those managers in the audience, would you now be listening?

3 *Be yourself*

The Problem

There are good presenters, and then there are others!

We all probably admire an effective presenter and find ourselves thinking: 'I wish I could copy her style in making a presentation. Clear, confident, persuasive – I hate her!' While there is nothing essentially wrong in trying to learn from people who are better presenters than us, the difficulties occur when imitation is taken too far.

On a presentation skills course some time ago, one participant gave a reasonable impression of a demented puppet (hopping around, waving arms, and so on). At first we thought it was nerves, but in fact he was doing it when he *remembered* to do it! When asked why he did it, he told us that he had a boss (a sales manager) who, when presenting, had a style rather like a preacher in the old West (fire and brimstone, tub-thumping, hell and damnation, and so forth). The boss had told our chap that he was 'too boring and had to put some life into his presentation', so . . .

Our course delegate was therefore trying (very badly) to copy someone else, and it simply did not work!

The Solution

Learn from others, by all means, but *do not copy them*. Develop your own style and, above all, be yourself! Try to capitalize on your strengths.

Analyse your weaknesses and work out how to correct and counter them in a way with which *you* are comfortable. Once our course participant did this, he was able to make his presentations far more interesting without resorting to hopping around and arm-waving.

IDEA 4

Work in
'bite-sized chunks'

The Problem

Years ago now, we had the misfortune to sit through a presentation lasting nearly three hours . . . without a break! By the end, 'nature' was in desperate straits and the style of seating meant that rigor mortis had reached an advanced stage. Those problems apart, much of the information was not absorbed because we (and probably everyone else there) had gone into 'work overload'. The sad part is that much of the information presented was relevant and interesting – but there was far too much of it!

So how does one impart the information without sending the audience into 'overload'?

The Solution

Most people's span of concentration seems to be around the 20 minute mark. After that, their attention usually deteriorates rapidly.

The solution is to accept that time scale as fact and operate accordingly by breaking the information down into manageable chunks. Try to keep the explanation of 'blocks' of information to 15 minutes maximum, then allow time for people to think about it and ask questions. If you *have* to give a long presentation, organize a break at least every hour!

For example, you have to inform a group about a new computer system. The breakdown of a one-hour presentation might look like this:

● Difficulties with the present 'manual' system (15 min.)

● Description of the main features of the new computerized system (15 min.)

- Break (5 min.) – coffee?
- How people will be trained in the use of the new system (10 min.)
- Questions about the system and/or training (15 min.)

IDEA 5 *'Pictures' are memorable*

The Problem

So many presentations seem to consist of purely verbal information or, if visual aids are used, copies of very complex charts or tables (often just copied from A4 sheets onto transparencies). Have you ever wished you had a pair of binoculars so you could actually *read* a transparency?

Perhaps people do not realize the difficulties such presentations cause, or, worse, they can't be bothered to do them properly. The problem of too much verbal data is caused by unawareness and can easily be cured, but there is no excuse for poor charts, tables and transparencies, which only serve to waste the presenter's time and that of the others they expect to understand them.

As we noted in an earlier chapter, 'One picture speaks a thousand words'.

If we are trying to make a point, which will have more impact: throwing a series of accident statistics at you or the picture shown here?

might just avoid

A Seat Belt is VITAL - make sure it is used!

The Solution

Most people appear to remember 'pictures' better than words, provided that the picture is relevant. Showing someone a picture of a new piece of large equipment will be more memorable than simply talking about it! The same applies to *easy-to-understand* graphs. For example, a simple pie chart of costs versus income will often make the main point and be remembered by the audience. 'But what about those people who want the detailed breakdown?' you might ask. No problem here. Have available secondary overheads showing detail in an easy-to-read form and/or an A4 handout with the detail as an appendix.

IDEA 6

Remember the three Ts

The Problem

A basic failing in far too many presentations is that the audience have no idea what to expect! They are never told why the presentation is being given, what will be covered, or how long it will take. In short, they are totally in the dark.

The presenter may know where he or she is going but it doesn't occur to them to let the audience know. A very brave member of the audience might ask: 'Where is this going?' or 'What is the point of this?' but that is extremely rare. They are far more likely to sit tight and hope that the purpose will eventually become clear. When it does, they then have the task of trying to think back over the previous 10 or 20 minutes to try and remember the essential information.

Whether you are trying to impart information or persuade, the audience must understand the objective and the relevance of what you are saying *early on*, otherwise it makes no sense, at least until later. Sometimes that 'later' is too late – the presenter has already lost the audience!

The Solution

We call this solution the 'three Ts' and it goes as follows:

> Tell them what you are going to tell them, then tell them, then tell them what you have told them.

This is an old adage and we have no idea how it originated. Suffice to say that it works, and works well!

We suggest that you apply this method to all your presentations – possibly with one or two slight additions – as follows:

157

1 Tell them what you are going to tell them (the objective, why you are talking to them, how you will get there, and for how long they will have to listen).

2 Tell them (logical structure and keep to the point).

3 Tell them what you have told them (in summary form containing: first, essential items of information they must remember; and secondly, your proposal and the chief benefits to them of adopting it).

Cover the snags as well as the benefits

IDEA 7

The Problem

We all have pride of authorship in our ideas: that is, we thought up the proposal, there are significant benefits to be gained from adopting it, and we are going to 'sell' it for all it's worth! Nothing wrong with that, you might think – you *have* to believe in something to sell it well. Agreed, but some people become almost evangelical about their proposal and lose sight of reality.

We have given this problem a name: 'the rose-tinted glasses' problem. In other words, in their enthusiasm for their idea, some people only ever state the benefits of the proposal and will never admit to any snags. Why?

Their behaviour stems mainly from a belief that mentioning the snags will diminish their case! Years ago, we knew a director who always used to ask 'OK so far, but what are the risks?' We lost count of the number of times he was told 'Oh, you've heard about those, have you?' Now that diminishes the case, in our view.

How would *you* react to two proposals, in the first of which the proposer enthusiastically quotes only the benefits, and in the second, the proposer outlines both the benefits *and* the snags?

The Solution

It is possible to cover both the benefits and the snags of the proposal and still be enthusiastic. You should be able to prove that the snags are outweighed by the benefits – otherwise why on earth are you presenting the proposal at all? This gives an objective view of the proposal and is likely to indicate to the 'approver' that you have considered both sides of the matter. You should also show how the snags can either be eliminated or reduced.

159

IDEA 8
Anticipate tough questions

The Problem

Have you ever seen an otherwise excellent presentation disintegrate during the 'question' stage at the end? Not much fun when it happens.

Some presenters seem to adopt the 'ostrich' principle during preparation. They bury their heads in the sand and ignore potentially tough questions in the hope that they will not arise, which is very dangerous thinking. Ignoring tough questions does not usually stop them. In fact, it might generate even more – when someone has their back to the wall, folk with a sadistic streak will try to make life even more difficult.

The Solution

At the preparation stage of a proposal, consciously consider the *very worst questions* that can be asked and decide whether:

1 they should be raised and answered by you during the presentation; or

2 they should be left to the audience to raise at the end.

In the first case, build the questions and your answers into the content of the presentation. In the second case, decide broadly what your answers will be if these questions come up.

If the circumstances are unfamiliar and you are unsure what questions could arise, try asking someone who has some knowledge in this or a similar field, and encourage them to generate the worst questions they can think of – no punches pulled. Often, asking your own manager might help – he or she has probably been in a similar situation.

As we have said before, if a question arises to which you do not know the answer, say so! Add when you *will* go back to them with an answer, and make sure that you do it.

IDEA 9
Remember to ask for approval

The Problem

The objective is to gain acceptance for a proposal, so let's look at what can easily happen. The proposal is clear, the advantages and benefits have been well stated, the risks are minor and can be easily handled, and the proposer finishes with a good summary of key points and answers well any questions that arise. Nothing wrong up to this point – as far as it goes. However, the proposer usually *leaves now to await the response later*. He or she therefore has no further opportunity to influence the outcome.

The problem is that most people seem afraid of asking: 'Now you have heard the idea, can I go ahead with it?' Why does this reticence occur? Basically, it is due to a fear of rejection. Nobody likes being told 'No!' But is that any reason for not asking? Is being told 'No' so bad?

The Solution

At the end of your presentation, remember to *ask for approval*: 'I have outlined why I think we should . . . Can I go ahead?'

Let's look at the possible responses from the 'approver':

- 'No.' This is the response that everyone fears. You can ask 'Why?' and attempt to handle the objection there and then. Taking the worst case, however, that the reason for 'No' is one you can't counter, at least you have learned something for next time.
- 'I like the idea but . . . ' Clarify the 'but . . . ' and see if you can find a way of handling it.
- 'Yes' in which case you have achieved what you wanted and can proceed with the proposal.
- 'Give me a couple of days to think about it.' If the proposal has far-reaching implications, this is quite reasonable. Set a date for the next meeting at which the answer will be given.

Make time for a dummy run

The Problem

Everyone has probably had to sit through an ill-prepared presentation at some time or other. Not much fun, is it? What are the signs? Unclear objective, no real structure, poor or inappropriate visual aids, rambling delivery, no real thought for what the audience wants, running out of time, and so on.

Some years ago we heard from a director a tale in which the board had told ten senior managers to prepare a 15-minute presentation outlining budget requirements for the coming financial year. Because of the number of presentations, the managers were told that the 15-minute deadline was mandatory. All of the managers except one stuck to this time limit and broadly obtained what they asked for (give or take 10 per cent). The manager who tried to overrun was stopped before he even reached his main point. Not surprisingly, he received significantly less than he wanted. He complained bitterly to his director saying that his presentation had taken far longer than he had anticipated. The director asked quietly, Did you do a dummy run?' Exit shame-faced manager stage left!

The Solution

In Idea 8.1, we talked about the importance of good preparation. If at all possible, ensure that you do a dummy run . . . to your partner, a colleague, to the mirror if necessary – any 'audience' will suffice. Even with good preparation, the *actual delivery always seems to take longer than we expect*. The dummy run should show up this problem and allow us to rectify it (and help to reduce the natural nerves).

Also remember 'Contingency Plan 1': have available a summary OHP slide showing just the main points of your proposal in case you do find yourself in danger of overrunning any deadline you have been given.

Summary

How to present information and proposals

- Nerves are *normal*.
- Gain their interest early.
- Be yourself.
- Work in 'bite-sized chunks'.
- 'Pictures' are memorable.
- Remember the three Ts.
- Cover the snags as well as the benefits.
- Anticipate tough questions.
- Remember to ask for approval.
- Make time for a dummy run.

Points to remember

_____

_____

_____

_____

_____

_____

_____

_____

9 How to run effective meetings

Ask people how they feel about meetings and in most cases there is a negative reaction, usually because people don't feel that the meetings they attend actually achieve very much.

Back in 1960, Richard Harkness defined a 'committee' as a group of the unwilling, picked from the unfit, to do the unnecessary. Unfortunately, some meetings can seem just like that, but they don't have to be. By using a few fairly simple guidelines, meetings can be productive and fun to be involved with.

The objectives for this chapter

After reading this chapter, you should know and understand:

- How to decide if a 'meeting' is the best means of achieving the objective.

- Why meetings should be results-oriented.

- Some main principles that will help you to run effective meetings.

Defining a meeting

We define a 'meeting' – as distinct from what we would call a conference – as: 'an exchange of ideas, information, or opinions by a group of people with an active role to play, to achieve specific results'. We are not talking here about conferences of 100 people where most of the audience are in a passive role, listening to a series of speakers.

Why results-orientation is important to successful meetings

Coming out of our research, the most frequent criticism of meetings is that 'they don't achieve much'.

People are quite prepared to put effort into a meeting if they can see a definite result coming out of it. But it is extremely frustrating to 'do your homework', input effectively, and then find that there is no real specific outcome. 'We only talked. Nothing was decided!' If this happens, it's not too surprising that the reaction to another invitation is: 'Not another meeting – what a waste of time!'

Is a meeting the best way?

The Problem

Some managers seem automatically to call a meeting if there is anything to discuss, without ever appearing to consider whether a meeting is actually the best way to communicate.

Have you ever been in a meeting where a significant proportion of it was a conversation between the chairperson and one or two other participants? Quite frequently the others are wondering why they have to sit there for 20 minutes listening to something that is irrelevant (to them) and which could have been handled via a telephone call or a smaller meeting.

Another aspect of this problem concerns information giving. Some people call a meeting to impart information that could easily be sent out in written form. A good example of this would be a revised but straightforward procedure. If no discussion or clarification of the procedure is necessary, why call a meeting?

The Solution

Decide what the objective(s) are and then determine the best method of achieving each one. The following options are obvious but often do not seem to be considered:

- Send out written information with the option to ask questions if necessary.

- Phone call.

- One-to-one discussion.

- Subgroup meeting, with specific objectives.
- Full group meeting, again with specific objectives.

Often a full group meeting is *not* the best way of communicating, but it is the method that some people *always* seem to use!

The agenda should show results-oriented objectives, rather than subjects

IDEA 2

The Problem

An agenda for a meeting is intended not only as a checklist for the chairperson, but also to help participants to prepare for the meeting. If you have one, look at an old meeting agenda. Most agendas seem to be based on subjects rather than objectives, so that the content may read as follows:

● Minutes of the last meeting.

● Progress on computer project.

● Lunch-time phone cover.

● Improving communications.

● Any other business.

This would undoubtedly remind the chairperson of the subjects to be covered and in what order, but if you were to receive that agenda as a participant, could you adequately prepare for the meeting? Unless you knew all the background to each of the headings, probably not.

Participants also want a meeting to achieve results (usually), but with this type of agenda they can only guess at the underlying intention.

169

The Solution

Set result-oriented objectives. For example, based on the original agenda above:

- Confirm that actions agreed at the last meeting have been taken.
- Decide actions, individual responsibilities and deadlines for phase 3 of the computer project.
- Set up and agree a workable rota for lunch-time phone cover in our department.
- Decide how to find out regularly how our customers (internal and external) feel about the service we provide and decide who will do what.

This type of agenda will probably lengthen the meeting, but the results will be worth it.

Eliminate 'Any other business' from agendas

The Problem

Do you attend or run meetings that contain 'Any other business' (AOB) on the agenda? If not, congratulations – you don't need this idea. However, if your meetings *do* contain this item at the end, this idea can save you much time (and grief).

AOB is there to allow time to cover any additional issues that participants may want to discuss which are not listed on the agenda. What typically happens though? Often all the rubbish that nobody can find a home for appears under that heading (we call it the 'dustbin slot'). Frequently you find that the same old subjects come up every time: for instance, Harry moaning about his wobbly chair (for the ninth time). Even when 'sensible' issues are brought up, the rest of the group had no pre-warning and therefore often lack the necessary information to contribute to the discussion. Thus the next ten minutes is spent deciding that nothing can be decided (yet). Very productive, don't you think?

The Solution

If you are the chairperson, encourage people to let you have *their* objectives before the agenda is finalized.

Tell them that, as of the next meeting, AOB will no longer exist. If there are any issues they want included for discussion, they must let you have the *objective* before the agenda is finalized, together with an estimate of the time they think the issue is worth. If a genuine 'crisis' item occurs immediately prior to the meeting, then either agree to extend the meeting time or drop a less important item.

If you are a participant, you might be able to suggest the idea of removing AOB privately to the chairperson.

Start your meetings on time

IDEA 4

The Problem

First impressions do count! People learn very quickly whether or not your meetings start on time, and usually act accordingly. First one person comes in ten minutes late, next time three people will be fifteen minutes late, and so it progresses.

Often the chairperson has to delay discussion of an item (because the latecomer's input is needed) or call an unnecessary coffee break (they have only just finished the scheduled break) in order to make a frantic phone call.

When the latecomer does eventually arrive, what does the chairperson do? Summarizes! Consequently, the latecomer learns that when he or she is late they will be brought up to date – which positively encourages prompt attendance in future, doesn't it?

While all this is going on, what about the other people who did organize themselves well enough to be present for the start of the meeting? They are on *your* side, trying to help you by being there on time. Yet it is their time that is being wasted.

The Solution

After 'starting time' on the agenda, write 'sharp please' and ensure that you actually start your meeting at that time. People will quickly learn that you do mean it: 'Better go. Karen's meetings always start on time.'

When a latecomer arrives, decide whether the lateness is justifiable or not. If it is, by all means, summarize. If not, or it's becoming a habit, try ignoring them (apart from 'Hello, Ken . . . now what were you saying, Marion?') for about five minutes – then summarize. The short period of being ignored is uncomfortable for the latecomer (and they don't know that it will only be five minutes). In our opinion, you owe it to the people who took the trouble to be there on time not to let the latecomer's arrival disrupt them.

5 *Set a finish time*

The Problem

Do the meetings you attend have a declared finishing time? If they do, and these times are reasonably adhered to, then you don't need this idea. In our experience, however, few meetings are given a set finishing time, yet we all try to guess what that time is likely to be so that we can organize the rest of the day.

The main reasons why finishing times are not set for most meetings are as follows:

● No one thought of doing it.

● The chairperson has no idea how long the meeting will take.

● The chairperson does not want to stifle discussion artificially.

Have you ever sat in a meeting and wondered: 'How much longer is this going to take? We are talking it to death.' ?

The Solution

Most people view meetings with a declared finishing time as well organized and productive. It seems to focus the mind rather than stifle.

In order to establish a finishing time, it is necessary to estimate how long each objective on the agenda is *worth*. Estimating is guesstimating! The more you do it, the better you become at it. At first, until you become reasonably accurate at estimating, build in an extra 15 to 30 minutes to give yourself some cover on the items on which you are unsure. If you have no previous experience of estimating a meeting schedule, try asking someone who has a reputation as a good chairperson to give you some guidelines. They won't mind doing that!

One last point. Try not to hold meetings that last longer than two hours. People's concentration starts to wander after this.

While it is not always feasible, the two-hour guideline could be used far more often than it is. If you do have to hold a long meeting, build in breaks or consider holding shorter sub meetings on some of the items up for discussion.

Consider using a 'scribe' and a flipchart for clarity

The Problem

Do the minutes of a meeting you receive a week later sometimes bear little resemblance to the meeting you attended?

What typically happens is that the chairperson, who is usually also responsible for note-taking nowadays, scribbles furiously while trying to control the meeting as well. First, it is hard to perform both roles (chairperson and 'secretary') simultaneously – one or the other usually suffers. To take a cynical view, some chairpersons, if unsure, write down what they wanted to hear anyway! Secondly, people cannot see what is being written down on an A4 pad, so they don't know whether the note matches or even *relates* to what they have just said. It is not too surprising, therefore, that errors occur.

The Solution

Consider asking someone to act as 'scribe' and let them use a flipchart. The sheets can be easily torn off after the meeting and taken back. (Wipe-clean boards might be more environmentally friendly but can't be easily transported, especially if they measure 6 ft. × 4 ft. and are screwed to the wall!)

The 'scribe' will require some guidance as to exactly what to record (for example, who will do what by when), and the information is visible to everyone. If a mistake occurs it will be easily spotted and corrected.

177

You might even like to go one step further and issue the contents of the flipchart as 'minutes'. Often, most people only want to know what was decided, what has to be done, by whom, and by when. Try asking those at the meeting what they want the minutes to contain. Most will say 'Keep it simple!' – for internal meetings, at least.

Consider using a 'stand-in' Chair when you need to become involved in the content

IDEA 7

The Problem

A difficult dilemma occurs when a manager is chairing a meeting and also has to be a leading contributor to one or more agenda items. As a contributor, the need is to input/discuss information whereas, as chairperson, the role is to control the input and ensure that it is relevant to the objective(s).

There is a potential conflict between these two roles which is often hard to resolve. It is all too easy to talk far too much or drift away from the point. Furthermore, most people who attend meetings are reluctant to try and call the chairperson to order (especially if that person is their manager as well).

The Solution

Consider using a 'stand-in' to chair the section of the meeting where you need to act as a leading contributor. It is an excellent development opportunity for someone who is working towards a management position.

Two principles are important here.

1 Discuss the objective(s) with your 'stand-in' *before* the meeting to ensure that they understand what you are trying to achieve.

2 When handing over the chair *during* the meeting, explain that the 'stand-in' will control the next item(s), and that includes *your* input. You could even make a joke of it if you wish.

One final thought; if you have to be a prominent contributor thoughout most of the meeting, then why not let your 'stand-in' chair the whole meeting?

Pre-handle potential difficulties when (more) senior people attend your meeting

IDEA 8

The Problem

One problem that people frequently raise on the 'Meetings' courses that we run is: 'How do I, as chairperson, handle the situation where my boss (or someone else senior) turns up and proceeds to take over the meeting? It makes me feel surplus to requirements'.

This difficulty does not (usually) arise from rudeness but from two other factors:

1 Senior people are used to chairing meetings and therefore tend to fall naturally into the role without necessarily meaning to disrupt.

2 Those attending the meeting tend to address questions and comments to the most senior person present, rather than to the chairperson, especially if the senior person arrives unexpectedly.

The Solution

If you fear that this situation might occur (or already has occurred), try discussing it with the senior person involved *privately, one to one*. The past is gone but the idea is to *prevent future difficulties* for you, as chairperson. You might like to try the following approach:

- Constructively, explain how you felt and the difficulties it caused (or what you feel could potentially happen).

- Outline your objectives for the next meeting, and then find out what the senior person expects from the meeting.

- Ask the senior person to suggest how best to conduct the meeting in order to meet both sets of needs. Most senior people understand and are normally extremely helpful. You should then be able to decide between you on your respective 'roles' and agree an appropriate plan for the meeting.

Ensure that participants understand their role

IDEA 9

The Problem

Have you ever attended a meeting where you thought the objective was to *make* a decision, only to find that the decision is to be made by someone else and you were simply being *consulted*?

A recent example was at a meeting with an agenda item of 'new software'. The group thought that they were going to be asked to discuss requirements and *decide* what new software would be of benefit in the department, so they discussed possible useful additions before the meeting. As the meeting progressed, however, it became clear that the manager only wanted to *consult* them about their ideas so that *she* could decide on the final list, also taking into account the needs of a second section reporting to her. The group saw their role as 'decision making', but the manager saw their role as 'providing information', and this point was not clarified until 30 minutes into the agenda item.

The Solution

As we have said before, clear objectives are vital. However, even some seemingly clear result-oriented objectives may not make the role of the participants clear. Also, people are human – they occasionally misinterpret things!

As part of the introduction to *each objective* on the agenda, the chairperson should ensure that the role of the participants *is made clear*. The following questions on 'role' might help:

- Are they being consulted for their views prior to a decision elsewhere?

- Are they making the decision, or producing a recommendation?

- Are they discussing the implementation of a decision made elsewhere?

Get a definite commitment to act

IDEA 10

The Problem

Consider the following example. The meeting went well, and everyone seemed comfortable with the outcome and action plan. At the next meeting, progress is discussed and Fred suddenly commented: 'Well, I didn't actually agree to do that, you know. You just assumed that I would.' Back came the plaintive reply, 'But I'm sure you agreed to do that last time, didn't you?'

Most people try their best to take the necessary action by the given deadline. There are some, however, who seem to make a career out of avoiding any responsibility. They succeed in doing so because no one says specifically: 'Fred, will you take responsibility for . . . ?' Agreement is sometimes assumed: that is, if the person says nothing, it is assumed that he or she has accepted the consensus.

Action Plan			
What	Who	By when	**Agreed**
	—	—	✔
	—	—	✔
	—	—	✔

The Solution

The answer is to insist upon a *definite 'public' agreement* ('Yes' will do) by each person to take the relevant action by a specific date. Any disagreement must be resolved at that point.

This is made easier if you are using a flipchart with the 'what, who and by when' format (see Idea 9.6). The action plan should then be clear to everyone. To help in this situation, you can add a column headed 'Agreed' to the right of the 'What', 'Who' and 'By when' columns on the flipchart. Having produced the action plan, ask every person involved if they agree to the actions listed for them, and, on agreement, *tick the action item*. You may only be doing this in fact for one person (who always tries to wriggle out of responsibility), but it is important to apply it to all. You can easily explain it as helping you to check that you (or the 'scribe') have recorded all points accurately.

Summary

Running effective meetings

- Is a meeting the best way?
- The agenda should show results-oriented objectives, rather than subjects.
- Eliminate 'Any other business' from agendas.
- Start your meetings on time.
- Set a finish time.
- Consider using a 'scribe' and a flipchart for clarity.
- Consider using a 'stand-in' Chair when you need to become involved in the content.
- Pre-handle potential difficulties when (more) senior people attend your meeting.
- Ensure that participants understand their role.
- Get a definite commitment to act.

Points to remember

_____

_____

_____

_____

_____

_____

_____

10 How to help your people improve their performance

Helping people in your team to improve their performance involves performance counselling.

Now many managers seem to reserve performance counselling only for team members who are experiencing difficulties. Certainly helping someone whose performance is below the expected level is very important, but that is only one part of the overall picture. Every manager should be trying to help *everyone* in his or her team to improve their performance. After all, even the best can improve – and if you doubt that, try asking them! Often the high performers are the most eager to find ways of doing even better. They do not 'rest on their laurels', and that's why they are where they are.

Moreover, what about those in the team who are delivering a 'normal' level of performance? Should they not receive attention as well?

The objectives for this chapter

After reading this chapter, you should know and understand:

- What 'performance counselling' is.

- Why it is important.

- Some principles that will enable you to help your team members to improve their performance.

'Performance counselling'

The word 'counselling' means different things to different people, ranging from a chat by the coffee machine to a service that is only provided by a professional specialist.

'Performance counselling' is an attempt by the manager to help the individual to explore, identify and 'own' their performance strengths and weaknesses, and to enable them to find ways of capitalizing on the strengths and correct the weaknesses in order to improve their performance.

Why 'performance counselling' is important

Management involves 'getting results'; that's how most managers are measured. 'Getting results' means helping *all* the individuals in the team to operate at the highest performance level of which they are capable. 'Performance counselling' is an important tool for helping a manager achieve this requirement.

'Ownership' is vital

The Problem

Say there is a section leader in your team who staunchly refuses to delegate anything to people within their section. As a direct result, they are doing vast amounts of the more difficult routine work but are not doing the planning and distribution of work that is part of their role specification. You call them in to discuss the problem and they insist that they can do it quicker, better, and so forth, than their people. You tell them to try and delegate more, and you clearly explain how to start. Off they go, and what happens? Nothing! Because they sincerely did not believe that they were doing anything 'wrong' in the first place. They were simply doing their very best to produce the work from a busy section. In short, they did not 'own' the problem you had identified.

Telling someone that there is a problem does not mean they believe you. When you were a youngster and your mum or dad told you off for coming home late from a party, did you believe then that you had done anything wrong? 'They are being unreasonable.' 'They don't understand.' 'They are old' would all have been fairly typical reactions!

How do you make someone understand that there is a weakness (or, indeed, a strength) without actually *telling* them?

The Solution

By encouraging 'ownership': that is, by reaching a point where the individual personally accepts their strength or weakness. Ownership is best achieved via effective questioning. For example:

● What do you see as your strengths/areas for improvement?

- What are the benefits/likely consequences of that strength/weakness?

'But what if they still don't accept it?' Then rather than tell them, use factual evidence without being aggressive. 'Andrea, you say you get on well with everyone, but this morning you were having a very heated argument with Mark. You also had one with Karen on Monday.'

Review performance objectively – strengths are just as important as weaknesses

The Problem

Let us introduce you to two 'counselling' characters: Mr/Ms Teddy Bear and Mr/Ms Rhino.

- **Mr/Ms Teddy Bear** A very pleasant and understanding manager. Everything is rosy, all is going well, and the only form of 'counselling' they give you is to tell you what a super job you are doing and how important you are to the organization. As far as they are concerned you never ever do anything wrong and, if a problem does occur, they appreciate that it is all due to someone else, or the computer system, and so on.

- **Mr/Ms Rhino** A rather different proposition. Often bad tempered or grumpy, they 'charge' head-on at the least provocation! When they 'counsel' you, you wonder if you *ever* do anything right in their view. They seem to worry too much about minor shortfalls (for example, spelling mistakes in a report), yet give you no credit for getting the important things right (for example, doubling sales).

If you have had the misfortune to work for either character, you will know exactly how it feels! Most people want (and expect) feedback from their manager and they expect it to be objective – tell it as it really is!

The Solution

Make sure that the counselling discussion is objectively balanced. Every team member has strengths and weaknesses – it's called 'being human!' Ensure that in your discussion you cover:

- Strengths, and how they can be used even more.
- Areas for improvement, and how to achieve the improvement.

Use 'open' questions mainly

The Problem

A typical conversation between a well-meaning manager and a reticent team member:

Manager: 'Are things alright out there, then?'
Team member: 'Fine!'
Manager: 'Any problems with workload?'
Team member: 'No.'
Manager: 'Things OK at home, are they?'
Team member: 'Yes.'
Manager: 'Is the computer working properly?'
Team member: 'Yes, it's fine.'

And so it goes on.

This type of question only produces a 'Yes' or 'No' type answer. What has the manager learned? Not a lot!

When trying to counsel reticent people about their performance, managers can easily resort to this form of question in order to elicit *some* sort of response from the 'unwilling' team member. The trouble is that, while it makes the team member 'make noises', it provides no useful information.

The Solution

Ask 'open' questions mainly. Open questions usually start with 'what, where, when, who, how, or why' and they collect *useful information*. For example:

- 'What effect is the new computer system having?'

- 'Why do you think that is happening?'

- 'How do you think we could solve that?'

Probing questions *relate to specifics*. For example:

- 'Why do you think a training course is the answer?'

Offer options rather than advice

The Problem

On our training courses that include sessions on counselling, we always ask people to define what 'counselling' means to them, as managers. Probably 60 per cent of respondents include the word 'advice' in their definition. This is positive in the sense that they are genuinely trying to help, but there is a definite risk. Ask yourself what could happen if you give advice.

- If it is good advice on a simple issue, the team member is grateful for the help and the suggested action(s) works.

- If it is good advice, and the team member does not agree or believe in it, it might fail because there is no commitment to it.

- If it is inappropriate for that person/situation but the manager/team member doesn't realize this, then the advice is likely to go wrong. Who, then, is blamed?

People on the whole give advice because they are trying to help. The advice is often quite valid if it relates to something that the team member could not be expected to know (for example, who to see in order to learn more about the invoicing system). However, when the situation is more complex than that, there is a better (safer) way!

The Solution

Offer options rather than advice, and encourage the team member to do the choosing. For example: 'We have agreed that some basic computer training would help you. The options are an external course within a month, an internal course in four months, or spend time now with Fred who knows our system well. Which do you think would best fill the bill?'

5 *Respect pauses*

The Problem

In a difficult situation, we don't like pauses. There appears to be a correlation between pauses and what we call the 'comfort factor'. The more comfortable we feel in a given set of circumstances, the less pauses worry us.

Next time you are at home, say, with friends you have known for a long time, try a little observation exercise. Sitting in the lounge with a drink (after dinner maybe), chatting generally about nothing in particular, watch for pauses in the conversation. We think you will probably find that there are quite long pauses, yet nobody bothers about them or possibly even notices them. The relationships are strong enough for the pauses not to worry anyone present. We don't immediately think: 'I must say something because the conversation has dried up.'

Counselling is not always a 'comfortable' process (even when praising good performance), so the manager is concerned about pauses and *often tries to fill the gap*! For example: 'Well, Marion, how do you think we could tackle that? . . . (5 second pause) . . . 'I think perhaps we should revise the system.'

The Solution

Accept that pauses are necessary, and do not try to fill the silence.

Often the questions asked in a counselling session are tough, which means that people need thinking time. Try to resist the natural temptation to fill the silence. Ask the question, then have a drink of coffee if it helps. Remember that you need *their* answer, not yours!

Look at behaviour, not personality

The Problem

Some managers have a tendency to describe difficulties in 'personality' terms:

- 'Andrea has an attitude problem.'
- 'Mark is downright obstructive'.
- 'Damion lacks any sort of spark.'
- 'Camilla is far too aggressive.'

What's wrong with that, you might ask? Have you ever tried telling someone they are aggressive or obstructive? People do not take kindly to that sort of observation! A common response is: 'What do you mean, I'm obstructive?'

A personality trait is incredibly hard to change (ask any psychiatrist). If the person has a particular trait, the odds are that you will be unable to alter it. However, there is one aspect that *can* be changed – behaviour!

The Solution

Discuss *actual behaviour* rather than personality traits.

Consider how the difficulty shows itself. For example, what tells me that Mark is obstructive? The answer might be: 'Mark resists every change, can never see any good in any of them, and always starts by saying he won't do it.' Now we are making some progress. Mark's actual behaviour is much simpler to define than abstract personality traits and these instances can be discussed far more easily. The outcome will probably not change how he feels inside, but it should change the way he actually behaves. In other words, he might still *feel* obstructive, but that does not mean he has to *behave* obstructively.

Don't try to be an 'amateur psychologist'

The Problem

Every manager probably tries to understand the people in their team, but some go too far. They indulge in what we call 'amateur psychology'. Two dictionary definitions might help us to understand this term:

1 *'Amateur'* A person unskilled in a subject or activity.

2 *'Psychologist'* One who studies the mental make-up of an individual to identify what causes him or her to act as they do.

Playing around with the unknown can be very dangerous, yet some managers still do it! Would you try to fix a gas leak yourself? Probably not, unless you know what you are doing. Yet without any proper training, some managers draw deep, meaningful conclusions about what makes someone tick and then, even worse, go ahead and act on those conclusions. When asked if they in fact talked to the individual concerned, they reply: 'No need to. I know what makes him tick!' That is very questionable! Even professional psychologists who we know are unlikely ever to claim that (although we stand to be corrected by a couple of friends!). People are very complex, and *fully* understanding them and their motives is a difficult undertaking.

The Solution

Do not make wild assumptions about what *you* think makes *someone* else tick, and you will avoid falling into the 'amateur psychologist' trap!

Keep it simple. Ask people how they feel and what they believe would be the best action(s), and why. Then try to build on their responses, if possible. But be careful not to impose your (possibly incorrect) assumptions on people.

Don't try to solve 'outside work' problems

The Problem

Let us say that I work for you and my work rate has recently dropped by 30 per cent. We talk and you discover that the cause of this problem is my failure to understand adequately some new procedure that has been implemented in the department. With work-related causes of this kind, the solution is fairly straight-forward. You arrange for me to have some extra training on this new procedure, it works, and that is that! The circumstances are work-related, and you manage the department and have the necessary authority to act.

However, suppose the cause of this performance drop had turned out to be that my partner had left me a short time ago, and so my mind had not really been on my work at all. Now what? First, your role as my manager is now quite different in this situation. You have no direct authority outside work. Secondly, you can't 'solve' the problem, much as you might like to!

The Solution

First, remember that your team member has already paid you a significant compliment by confiding in you at all.

Having found out that the cause lies outside work, discuss with them what role they wish you to play, and decide if that 'role' is acceptable to you. For example, they may want you to act simply as a trusted and understanding listener. You cannot, and should not, attempt to solve their problem – only they can do that. As we have mentioned before (see Idea 10.4), don't advise! Ask them to outline the options, or you could suggest some options if they appear to be stuck, and then encourage them to make the choice. After that, set a date to talk with them again.

With regard to the effect on them of the difficulty at work, find out what *they* think might ease the burden. (It is all too easy to, say, offer time off, when that is the last thing they want.)

IDEA 9 Meet your people regularly

The Problem

What is the first thought most people have when the boss calls them into the office? Usually, 'What have I done this time?' or something similar. Unfortunately, most people react in this way because that's what previous experience tells them.

As we mentioned in the introduction to this chapter, some managers only ever counsel when performance is poor. Time is at a premium and these managers often see this approach as an effective use of their time. Consequently, it is not too surprising that people come to associate such discussions with some form of 'telling-off'.

Often, therefore, when the team member arrives at your office, he or she has already decided what is likely to happen and mind-sets like this are hard to overcome. In other words, they are on the defensive and expecting censure – not at all the right atmosphere in which to begin effective performance counselling!

The Solution

Try to meet every member of your team regularly (say, once a month) to discuss performance. Performance discussions (that is, performance counselling) then become the *norm* and the negative perception disappears. Some managers might retort that they can't afford that sort of time. We would suggest that you can't afford *not* to!

For example, you have a team of eight and spend one hour per month with each. First, is eight hours per month (or 5 per cent of your time) such an unreasonable commitment? Second, if you are helping each member of the team gradually to improve their performance to a greater or lesser extent, the time investment is well worth the result.

Find out when to use specialist help

IDEA 10

The Problem

Many managers find it extremely hard where counselling is required to know in some cases where to draw the line: 'Where should I stop and let people with more experience/knowledge take over?'

Some people feel that, as the manager, they should be able to cope with or help in all matters affecting their team members. In truth, they are being very unfair both to themselves and to their team members. Suppose, for instance, that a manager suspects that a team member is drinking too much and this has started to affect his or her work. The manager talks to the individual and they admit the problem, but say they can't stop even though they have tried. Now what?

This, or a comparable situation, is the sort of dilemma that might only arise once in maybe ten years, but when it does, many managers will find themselves at a total loss about what to do next. Not a comfortable feeling.

The Solution

Accept that there are some situations in which you, as a manager, simply cannot cope. You have neither the relevant expertise nor professional training to handle the situation effectively. In fact, if you try, you may do more harm than good! What, therefore, *should* you do?

First, if you don't already know, find out what your organization's policies are with regard to alcohol, drug abuse, and any other situations which might require specialist help. Ask your personnel people specifically what action should be taken by the manager in cases of this nature, and ensure that you follow their advice. Knowing *before the event* how to proceed is far better than discovering half-way through that you should not have done what you did!

Summary

Helping people improve their performance

- 'Ownership' is vital.
- Review performance objectively – strengths are just as important as weaknesses.
- Use 'open' questions mainly.
- Offer options rather than advice.
- Respect pauses.
- Look at behaviour, not personality.
- Don't try to be an 'amateur psychologist'.
- Don't try to *solve* 'outside work' problems.
- Meet your people regularly.
- Find out when to use specialist help.

Points to remember

_____

_____

_____

_____

_____

_____

_____

_____

11

How to carry out an effective appraisal

Some organizations use the term 'appraisal', others use 'performance review', to refer to a regular (three-, six-, or twelve-monthly) meeting where the manager and team member formally discuss the team member's performance during the period since the last formal discussion, and then set objectives for the coming period. Assuming that you have such a system, the term used to describe these meetings in your organization doesn't matter; the principles are the same.

If you do not have an appraisal or review system, then after reading this chapter, consider whether you should propose the idea. You may well feel, as we do, that the potential 'pay-off' is more than worth the effort.

The objectives for this chapter

After reading this chapter, you should know and understand:

- What an appraisal (or regular review) is.

- Why it is important.

- Some principles that will help you to prepare for and run effective appraisals or regular reviews.

An appraisal or regular review

An appraisal or regular review is a formal – that is, key points noted in writing – and regular discussion between the manager and team member to *jointly*:

- review the team member's performance over the period since the last appraisal/review;

- discuss his or her training needs in their current role and appropriate actions; and

- agree his or her key performance objectives for the coming period.

Some appraisal or review meetings also cover career development needs and actions, though some organizations now use a separate discussion for this aspect.

Why appraisals or regular reviews are important

The organization's objectives are achieved by the successful accomplishment of individuals' objectives. To do this, people need feedback and help. The manager also needs the opportunity to communicate and clarify the direction of the department and the standards required.

The benefits to the *manager* of an effective appraisal or review system for team members include:

- Performance improvement (reinforcing strengths and addressing areas for improvement).

- Motivation via objective feedback.

- Specific assessment of the team member's training needs in his or her current role.

- If applicable, identifying future career potential and addressing development needs.

The benefits of an effective appraisal or review system for the *team member* include:

- Providing the answer to 'How am I doing?'

- Personal involvement in training plans (and, if applicable, career development plans).

- A positive outcome due to reinforcement of strengths and a constructive approach to dealing with areas for improvement.

Avoid surprises by regular feedback during *the appraisal/* review period

The Problem

We join the conversation part way through the appraisal:

Manager: 'Over the last year, on ten out of twelve occasions, you were two weeks late with your monthly reports. That caused me serious problems, Mandy, as I had to guess at the figures for my summary report.'

Mandy: 'Sorry, but to be honest, I thought they were another of those forms that everyone has to complete but nothing is actually done with them . . . they just get filed.'

Manager: 'Well, if you saw the grief I get from our director, you would view them differently. They must be in on time in future – and make sure you do it without me having to chase!'

Mandy: 'Hold on a minute, Peter. Why on earth didn't you tell me all this ten months ago? Why leave it this long?'

Unfortunately, some managers only ever talk about performance difficulties *at the appraisal*. By then, it is usually too late to do anything useful (as in this example). This leaves the team member feeling that the time-lag is unfair, which doesn't help their motivation much!

How, then, do you avoid these nonproductive surprises at an appraisal?

The Solution

Avoid surprises by reviewing performance, on a regular basis, *during* the year.

If you adopt Idea 10.9, you will meet all your staff on a monthly basis. Thus, in the example on the previous page, if the manager had been doing this, the late reports would have been discussed when the problem first appeared. This action would have avoided nine recurrences of the problem – and the surprise at the appraisal!

Jointly agree performance objectives for the coming period

The Problem

There are managers who believe that their role in the appraisal or review is to adopt a 'commanding' stance and *tell* the team member what is expected of them in the coming year. They see the setting of performance objectives as a strictly managerial task and some also appear to believe that this approach reduces the chances of 'argument' by the team member. In brief, he or she won't be given the *chance* to argue!

This approach may well reduce 'argument', but is the team member committed to those objectives? Probably not! If you were that team member, what would you think?

There is also another facet to this problem. Some performance objectives are easily measured (for example, sales revenue, number of computer programs written, and so on), but others are less easy to define without discussion (for example, co-operation with other members of the team, providing advice to other departments, and so forth). The manager's criteria for 'co-operation', say, may be markedly different from that of the team member. Without discussion, the manager might well set a target that is seen by the team member as unreasonable (or even inappropriate).

The Solution

Jointly agree performance objectives with the team member.

Encourage them to produce their list of suggested objectives before the discussion. During the discussion, compare it with your own list. You will probably find that you already agree on perhaps 80 per cent, which only leaves 20 per cent to be resolved.

For any objectives that are hard to measure – for example, co-operation – try to define what indicates that co-operation is taking place. For instance, you might both agree that it means taking initiative for helping others in a crisis. In this way, both manager and team member know what is expected and how co-operation can be judged.

The rating scale must be right

The Problem

Some appraisal schemes use a scale to rate the individual's performance against objectives or criteria. Some of these rating scales can cause serious problems, and one such scale that is in relatively common use is the one which goes: excellent, good, fair, poor (or similar).

The difficulty with this type of rating is to define clearly what is meant by these words. Your definition of 'good' can easily be different from someone else's. For example, is a 'good' meal out one which is cheap, tasty, high-class, served promptly, all of these, none of these, or what? Suppose the team member feels they have delivered a 'good' performance and the manager would only rate it as 'fair'. There is the distinct likelihood here of argument on a point that is very difficult to quantify.

Also, some managers are tougher (or softer) than others: 'I never give "excellent". Nobody is that good!' or 'I will give all my people "good" because I don't want to demotivate anyone.' Neither of these observations is objective, and people do seem to expect accurate feedback on performance.

The Solution

Whatever the rating scale, it must be clearly defined so that the individual as well as the manager can accurately rate performance. You might like to compare a rating scale with which you are familiar with the following one:

1 Performs consistently above the expected level of performance.

2 Performs occasionally above the expected level of performance.

3 Achieves expected level of performance.

4 Performs below the expected level of performance.

Provided of course that 'expected level of performance' has been clearly defined, we strongly believe that this scale is far more effective than 'excellent', 'good', and so on.

IDEA 4 *Allow sufficient time*

The Problem

We are constantly amazed that so many managers (even experienced ones) appear still to believe that spending any more than about 15 to 20 minutes on an appraisal discussion is some form of 'time management sin': 'It doesn't take *me* long to tell them what I think of them and what they should be doing next year!'

Some managers regrettably view the appraisal or review as another 'personnel form' that has to be filled in, and consider that the less time they spend on it, the better! What a shame that they really do not understand the point. The appraisal or review is there to help them and their team member.

The appraisal discussion should, at the very least, cover performance over the preceding period, and objectives for the coming period and should definitely *not* be a 'tell' session by the boss! An effective appraisal or review requires the active involvement of both the manager and the team member. It therefore takes a reasonable time to carry it out properly. That time investment is more than worth it in terms of performance benefits and future motivation.

The Solution

Let us try to define 'reasonable time'. As a rule of thumb, estimate the time you think the appraisal or review discussion will take, and *then double it*!

You will probably not be too far out in reality. In our opinion, an effective discussion is unlikely to take less than one and a half hours. If that seems too long to you, ask yourself which makes better sense: 90 minutes of joint discussion that has a significant effect on performance and motivation; or 20 minutes of 'tell' which may well have little effect (or even a negative effect)?

Find out how they *think they* have done

The Problem

Another misconception that some managers have about appraisals or reviews is a belief that their role is to act as both judge and jury on the team member's performance over the preceding period: 'Well, Karl (a trainer, let's say), you have done extremely well with regard to the courses you have run, but I do think you could have made more use of the computer in the training you do and that needs to improve next year. OK?'

As we have said before, telling someone they have a particular strength or weakness does not mean that they will necessarily believe you! How would the manager look if Karl replied: 'No, Marion, that's not really fair. I looked at the use of computers five months ago and decided then that they were of little benefit with the type of training I do. I did in fact mention this at the time.'

Moreover this 'feedback' has not helped Karl to recognize *why* he has 'done well on courses', and has provided him with no positive advice as to *how* he might 'make better use of the computer'.

The Solution

Before the appraisal or review, ask the team member to consider how they think they have done:

- What has been done well, and why?
- What could be improved, and how?

During the discussion, you can compare your individual views and you will probably find that your individual perceptions are close in most of the areas. Agreement on these points is therefore easy. The time can then be spent discussing any areas where you differ and exploring together the 'whys' and the 'hows'.

Spend most of the time looking forward

IDEA 6

The Problem

Let's say an appraisal or review takes place in December 1995, covering performance during 1995 and objectives for 1996. How much time do you think would be spent looking at performance in 1995 compared with that spent looking at objectives for 1996?

We have asked many course delegates for their views on this question. Most people say around 70 to 80 per cent of the time is spent looking back and some 20 to 30 per cent looking forward.

Why do some managers spend 70 to 80 per cent of the time looking backwards?

There are two main reasons for it:

1 They have to review the entire year because few (or no) discussions have taken place *during* the period concerned.

2 It is easier to talk about what *has* happened in the past rather than what *should* happen in the future.

We also ask the course delegates what in their opinion the percentage split *should* be. Everyone says it should be *reversed*, that is, 20 per cent looking backwards and 80 per cent looking forwards.

The Solution

We can't change the past – it's gone – we can only learn from it! The future is where we need to look to encourage change for the better. Therefore:

- Review performance regularly throughout the period. The appraisal or review discussion need then only involve a *summary* of what has already been discussed.

- Encourage the team member to prepare for the appraisal or review discussion by thinking about their own performance during the period concerned.

These actions should enable you to spend most of the time during the discussion looking forward.

Agree joint action plans

IDEA 7

The Problem

Most appraisal or review systems call for action plans and refer to the need for these plans to be jointly agreed.

However, some managers take the view that the only person who is supposed to take any action as a result of an appraisal or review is the *team member*; they see no need for personal action or contribution on their own part. Having agreed with the team member that he or she should do certain things, these managers believe they have 'followed the procedure and their task is completed. They have missed the point!

Certainly any actions should be jointly agreed to ensure 'commitment' but most team members need some help from their boss to make things happen. Yet some managers are quite content to say: 'We have agreed that you need to learn about running departmental meetings, so how do *you* think *you* might obtain that information?' This puts the onus entirely on the team member to make things happen – and that is exactly how it feels to them. People should take some responsibility for their own development, but that does not preclude the manager from helping. The need is for a genuinely joint action plan.

The Solution

Change the question to: We have agreed that you need to learn about running departmental meetings, so how do you think *we* can best do that?'

The team member is now far more likely to say that they will do some reading or attend a course, and will possibly suggest that you should let them run one of your meetings and then give them some feedback afterwards. Joint action plans should be an agreed series of actions involving both the manager and the team member – the team member cannot do it *all* on his or her own.

Don't just file
the action plan

The Problem

If you are involved with appraisals or reviews, here are two questions for you:

1 Is an action plan produced?

2 What happens to it?

As we mentioned in Idea 11.7, most appraisal or review systems call for action plans to be produced – and some are excellent! So far so good, but now on to the second question. Unfortunately, some of these first-rate action plans are unceremoniously buried under 'Appraisal' in a dusty old filing cabinet, to be resurrected only at the next appraisal or review the following year. At that stage, some time will be spent bemoaning the fact that certain things should have happened: 'Oh dear, I was supposed to fix up a computer course for you, wasn't I?'

The action plan should be a 'living document', and the worst thing that can happen to it is to bury it somewhere. 'Planned' actions are soon forgotten!

The Solution

1 Give the team member a copy of the action plan and ask them to note specific dates etc. in their diary.

2 Copy each action plan (the original usually has to stay with the appraisal or review documentation) and put them straight into a bring-forward file, so that each one surfaces at the right time for action.

If you have adopted monthly meetings with your team, consider reviewing progress on the action plan at those meetings.

Avoid 'Let's put you on a training course'

The Problem

'Hang on', you might reasonably think. 'Shirley and John run management training courses for a living. Are they really saying avoid training courses?' No, of course we are not against training. However, *training* should fulfil a specific need and a *course* should be the most appropriate way of meeting that need.

Nevertheless, readiness by some managers to 'put them on a course' is not *necessarily* the right answer to a need. It is, though, often the *easy* option, or it may even be a way of avoiding responsibility, a 'cop-out'! The sort of reasoning behind this 'cop-out' would be: 'I'm not sure how to tell him he is highly aggressive with everyone, so let's send him on an interpersonal course and perhaps they will tell him.' What the individual would be told by the manager, however, is: 'We are looking at this course for use by the company. Go along and see what you think.' The fact is that the course is unlikely to help unless the person knows the real reason why he or she is there and wants to learn from it.

Moreover, a course might not even be the best, or only, way. There are other alternatives to consider.

The Solution

Don't *automatically* suggest a course! Try to discuss the training need(s) objectively – that is, actual lack of knowledge, behaviour not personality. (If you are unsure about doing this, read Chapter 10 for some ideas that will help.)

Discuss which of the following approaches – and you may well know of others – would best meet the need, remembering that more than one approach might be required.

- Short training course (internal or external)
- Coaching by manager
- Longer-term learning
- Coaching by colleague/trainer
- Reading company-produced information
- 'Shadowing' (observing the manager)

Consider 'upwards appraisal'

The Problem

Few managers receive any real feedback from their team, and still fewer actually encourage it!

Ask yourself how you feel about the prospect of telling your own manager what he or she does well and what you believe he or she could do to improve the working relationship with you. Your answer probably depends very much on how well you 'get on' with your current manager. It seems that the better managers encourage feedback from their team, but often the team feel that their manager does not need it.

It's the 'bad' managers who do need feedback, but they never ask! Some have not even considered it. Others fear that they might stir up a nest of hornets that they won't be able to handle, and none of us (probably) likes pain much! Still others might feel that they would 'lose respect' if they allowed criticism (as they see it) – they don't understand that taking notice of constructive criticism *increases* respect.

The problem revolves around encouraging constructive feedback from the people in your team

The Solution

Consider what we term 'upward appraisal'. This concept involves you in choosing people whose views *you* respect and who you believe will give you useful feedback, and then asking directly for their views.

'In order to improve even more the way in which we work together:

- What do you think I, as your manager, do well and why?
- What do you think I, as your manager, could improve and how?
- What actions should we take?'

Aim to encourage balanced, useful (constructive) feedback, and *listen*!

Summary

Carrying out an effective appraisal

- Avoid surprises by regular feedback *during* the appraisal/review period.
- Jointly agree performance objectives for the coming period.
- The rating scale must be right.
- Allow sufficient time.
- Find out how *they* think they have done.
- Spend most of the time looking forward.
- Agree *joint* action plans.
- Don't just *file* the action plan.
- Avoid 'Let's put you on a training course'.
- Consider 'upwards appraisal'.

Points to remember

_____

_____

_____

_____

_____

_____

_____

_____

Conclusion

In the introduction to this text, we explained that we have attempted to outline some basic, but nevertheless very important, ideas to help across a wide range of management activities.

Whether you have read the entire book, or selected relevant chapters, we hope that you have gained some useful ideas from your reading.

Please don't leave them here, however, where they will remain only as 'good ideas' and nothing more. You have probably put considerable time and effort into your reading and it is important that you achieve some real benefit from that activity.

Apply the 80:20 rule to what you have learned. Decide which ideas are going to be of most significant use to you *now*, and then decide *how* and *when* you will implement them. Don't try to implement too much all at once.

If you should find yourself on one of our management skills or communication skills courses one day, we look forward to seeing you and will be happy to discuss any of the ideas in this book with you. Should you have any queries, our telephone number is 01604 – 491230.

Meanwhile, we hope our advice has been of interest and assistance to you. Our best wishes to you in your management tasks and responsibilities.

Bridging the Performance Gap

Dr Trevor J Bentley

Does your organization suffer from 'the performance gap'? The chances are that you have managers and staff who - on paper at least - have all of the competencies and experience to do a really good job. Why is it then that some of them never seem to fulfil their true potential?

The fact is that we all need to be competent to perform but competency is no guarantee of a successful outcome.

Bridging the Performance Gap is a practical guide to effective performance management that enables you to:

• identify the missing ingredients in an individual's performance
• measure the gap between performance and potential
• develop skills, techniques and systems to: encourage learning; support personal development; review, recognize and reward performance improvement.

Trevor Bentley shows you how to release the latent potential of everyone within your organization through a process of encouragement and support that relies on bringing a human TOUCH (Trust, Openness, Understanding, Consideration, Honesty) to everything that they do. *Bridging the Performance Gap* offers a complete and effective strategy for making this work for the benefit of you, your people, and your organization.

| 1996 | 200 pages | 0 566 07760 4 |

Gower

How to Make Work FUN!

An Alphabet of Possibilities ...

David Firth

With the majority of our lives spent either at work or asleep it seems crazy to consign 'fun' only to life outside of the office. Why do we leave our personalities behind when we set off for work in the morning? Why do we envy people who tell us that their work is fun, yet somehow feel laughter is out of place in the office? And how can we deliver excellent service, or be better than our competitors, if we'd rather not be working at all?

David Firth's totally irreverent book is packed with ideas for banishing boredom and bringing fun to the office. And building stronger teams and increasing productivity in the process ... Find out why you should persuade your company to train your team how to juggle, the benefits of practising saying phrases such as: "Does anyone think that I am bullshitting?", or "Does anybody here know a good joke?", seven new venues for efficient meetings, and what 'KIT' stands for, and why it's a good idea!

This book is a must for anyone who'd like to foster a team spirited positive working environment, get work into perspective (reduce stress levels), or simply enjoy work more. It should be studiously avoided by anyone who feels threatened by the very idea of deriving fun from work.

1995   224 pages   0 566 07712 4

Gower

It's Not Luck

Eliyahu M Goldratt

A Gower Novel

Alex Rogo has had a great year, he was promoted to executive vice-president of UniCo with the responsibility for three recently acquired companies. His team of former and new associates is in place and the future looks secure and exciting. But then there is a shift of policy at the board level. Cash is needed and Alex's companies are to be put on the block. Alex faces a cruel dilemma. If he successfully completes the turnaround of his companies, they can be sold for the maximum return, but if he fails, the companies will be closed down. Either way, Alex and his team will be out of a job. It looks like a lose-lose situation. And as if he doesn't have enough to deal with, his two children have become teenagers!

As Alex grapples with problems at work and at home, we begin to understand the full scope of Eli Goldratt's powerful techniques, first presented in *The Goal*, the million copy best-seller that has already transformed management thinking throughout the Western world. *It's Not Luck* reveals more of the Thinking Processes, and moves beyond *The Goal* by showing how to apply them on a comprehensive scale.

This book will challenge you to change the way you think and prove to you that it's not luck that makes startling improvements achievable in your life.

1994   288 pages   0 566 07637 3

Gower

The New Unblocked Manager

A Practical Guide to Self-development

Dave Francis and Mike Woodcock

This is unashamedly a self-help book, written for managers and supervisors who wish to improve their effectiveness. In the course of their work with thousands of managers over a long period the authors have discovered twelve potential "blockages" that stand in the way of managerial competence. They include, for example, negative personal values, low creativity and unclear goals.

By means of a self-evaluation exercise, the reader first identifies the blockages most significant to them. There follows a detailed explanation of each blockage and ideas and materials for tackling the problem.

This is a heavily revised edition of a book that, under its original title, *The Unblocked Manager*, was used by many thousands of managers around the world and appeared in ten languages. The new edition reflects the changed world of management and owes much to the feedback supplied by practising managers. In its enhanced form the book will continue to provide a comprehensive framework for self-directed development.

1996   264 pages   Hardback 0 566 07639 X   Paperback 0 566 07705 1

Gower

Practical NLP for Managers

Ian McDermott and Joseph O'Connor

It is almost a truism to say that your success as a manager depends on the quality of your communication.

NLP (Neuro-Linguistic Programming) is based on the study of excellence and provides the most powerful tools currently available for improving communication skills. There are many books setting out the relevant techniques; this is the first to show them at work in a practical management setting. The authors, both of them experienced NLP trainers, look in turn at each of the key elements in the management process and show how NLP can help. They explain

- how to capture other people's attention and trust
- how to motivate
- how to use language (including body language) to maximum effect
- how to handle staff appraisals
- how to develop a consistent set of organizational values.

Practical NLP for Managers is a powerful communication skills tool for every manager who wants to improve their powers of persuasion and leadership.

1996   224 pages   0 566 07671 3

Gower

Problem Solving for Results

Victor Newman

In this thought-provoking book Dr Newman looks beyond the conventional techniques of problem solving to the underlying process. He identifies eight stages and explains how to recognize which technique is appropriate to which stage. On this basis managers can generate solutions at both the personal and the organizational level.

He shows:

- how to overcome the four main obstacles to developing a balanced problem solving style
- how to manage the relationship between problem solving style and stress
- how to use physical movement as an aid to problem solving.

A unique feature of the book is a Problem Solving Styles Profile that enables each reader to apply the material in the text to improve their own problem solving capability.

Written in a lively and practical style and drawing on examples from a wide range of real-life problems, Dr Newman's book is certain of a warm welcome from managers, team leaders and professionals of every kind.

1995   158 pages   0 566 07566 0

Gower

The Turbocharged Company

Igniting Your Business to Soar Ahead of the Competition

Larry Goddard and David Brown

Imagine, for a moment, that the business you own or work for is so successful that you cannot wait to get there each day. Sales are better than planned, and costs are on the decrease; the company's making money in a competitive marketplace, whilst providing exceptional value to your customers. All staff are productive and dedicated; customers write to applaud your service, not to complain.

Sounds too good to be true? But what if it could be a reality for your organization?

Goddard and Brown set out to find out how a handful of US companies stood head and shoulders above the rest. They looked at nearly 1,000 of the largest US businesses, and identified just 3% that they described as 'turbocharged' - all had outperformed their closest competitor by more than 40% over three years. All had somehow turned a level playing field into a significant competitive advantage. But how? On the face of it, they subscribed to a wide range of different business philosophies.

In this book, the authors identify the common factors - the 'turbocharged process' that put these companies out of the reach of their rivals. This total approach to business success incorporates a range of strategies such as TQM, ISO 9000, Benchmarking and Statistical Process Control (SPC), but is based on four essential foundations:

- unleashing people power
- Not just listening to, but revering your customers
- relentlessly pursuing productivity
- focusing on strengths, and on being the leader in your field.

Packed with examples from America's turbocharged companies, this book will help you build these foundations and get ahead of your competitors.

| 1996 | 320 pages | 0 566 07813 9 |

Gower

The Vision

Richard Israel and Julianne Crane

In the new global economy, where wealth is information and the rules of business have been turned inside out, a new force is emerging. It weighs three pounds, works 24 hours a day and has unlimited potential. Sounds like you should find out more? Well, you're already the proud owner of one. In fact, you are using it now.

Recent research has begun to reveal the mysteries of the human brain and its almost infinite capacity. *The Vision* provides a step-by-step guide to using more of your creative genius. It tells the fast-moving story of Sandy Stone, as she struggles to boost the performance of her sales team, battles with her unhelpful boss, teaches – and learns from – her young son. As you share Sandy's experiences you will learn with her:

- how to create and achieve a peak sales vision for more sales
- how to harness the power of your brain
- how to use multi-sensory thinking
- how to mind-map for improved memory and recall
- how to become a visionary leader
- how to change limiting belief systems (your own and other people's)
- how to enhance self-esteem, and how to manage your time more effectively
- how to master the visionary process for future growth.

The story is followed by a commentary in which the authors explain the key learning points in more detail.

| 1996 | 150 pages | 0 566 07797 3 |

Gower